I've known Tyler Feller for several years now, and I can tell you that no one is more qualified to write on this topic. He has faced so many challenges in life with gratitude and grit. And through it all, he's never stopped. I know you will be greatly blessed as you keep going each day this year with this devotional as a guide.

Alex Himaya, senior pastor, BattleCreek Church;
author, *Jesus Hates Religion*

In *Don't Stop: 365 Daily Devotions to Ignite Your Purpose*, Feller offers questions to awaken your thoughts, biblical insights to stir your spirit, and practical direction to keep you moving forward so you may step into a powerful future with our triune God. In 365 days, you will be not only ignited but launched into a new dimension of faith and purpose. You may even be unstoppable!

Dr. Kim Maas, founder and CEO, Kim Maas Ministries; author,
Prophetic Community, The Way of the Kingdom, and *Finding Our Muchness*

Don't Stop by Tyler Feller is a powerful book that will inspire and guide you on a yearlong journey of purpose and fulfillment. No one can speak to this subject better than Tyler, and this book is a must-read for anyone seeking to embrace each day with renewed passion and purpose.

Mike Signorelli, lead pastor, V1 Church

Rooted in Christian principles, *Don't Stop* will guide you toward the realization that you were created for something far greater than mere existence. Its pages are brimming with the spiritual nourishment necessary to turn your thoughts and actions toward the Creator. In a world that often urges us to settle for the ordinary, *Don't Stop* will lead you to view challenges as opportunities and setbacks as stepping stones. Let it awaken your spirit, fuel your passion, and guide you toward the life you were destined to lead.

Brian Simmons, cofounder, Passion & Fire Ministries

Tyler Feller is a friend and incredibly gifted by God in the areas of creativity and entrepreneurial enterprise. He lives not according to his past but according to the Word of God and his intimate connection with Jesus Christ. Tyler has partnered with the Holy Spirit and scripted an invitation for every reader to do what the

Lord has taught Tyler to do: daily overcome the obstacles that confound you through dynamic faith and step into the discovery process of who you were born to be.

Reverend Joanne Moody, president and cofounder, Agape Freedom Fighters

I am so pleased that Tyler Feller has written this excellent daily devotional. This devotional will challenge you to live out God's Word, and it will enhance your advancement in strategic areas of your life. This devotional will bless many as they reflect on God's Word and apply it to their lives. Thank you, Tyler, for your labor of love and this gift to the body of Christ.

Connie Dawson, PhD, professor of church and revival history, Global Awakening Theological Seminary

Tyler masterfully weaves together timeless truths, contemporary relevance, and divine inspiration, creating a tapestry of spiritual growth and renewal. As a fellow believer, I can confidently say that *Don't Stop* has enriched my spiritual walk and deepened my relationship with God. It is an invitation to embrace the sacredness of each moment while drawing you closer to the divine and illuminating your path to grace and purpose.

Doug Bishop, founder, United Search Corps

Tyler Feller's *Don't Stop* devotional is a great way to start the day. Each day it helps you get closer to your dreams by providing step-by-step guidance based on Scripture. Tyler asks thought-provoking questions that will help you fulfill all that God has for you.

Dr. Geoff Wattoff, adjunct professor, Global Awakening Theological Seminary; author, *Restoring the Soul*

Tyler Feller's love for Jesus and the world is truly inspiring. There are times in life when our walk with God can be tough, and it can be even tougher to remind ourselves what he calls us to do. Tyler hits the sweet spot with this devotional as he walks us through how we can continue pursuing our calling and staying motivated while combating the doubtful ways of the world.

Russell Horning, Backpack Kid; inventor, Floss Dance

don't stop

365 Daily Devotions
to Ignite Your Purpose

TYLER FELLER

BroadStreet
PUBLISHING

BroadStreet Publishing® Group, LLC
Savage, Minnesota, USA
BroadStreetPublishing.com

Don't Stop: 365 Daily Devotions to Ignite Your Purpose

9781424567263 (faux leather)
9781424567270 (ebook)

Cover and interior by Garborg Design Works | garborgdesign.com

Printed in China

24 25 26 27 28 5 4 3 2 1

foreword

Tyler Feller is a man with a heart for God. Since I first met Tyler, I have been impressed with his heart, intellect, and spirit. I have seen him put God first while rejecting several offers that many a Christian would have been tempted to say yes to—very good opportunities that would not have been the will of God. Tyler, however, looked at the opportunities by asking, "Will this bring me closer to Jesus? Will I become a stronger Christian, a wiser leader? Will this decision position me to make a greater impact on my generation, the millennials?"

He has been a student in several of my classes at the seminary where I am president, Global Awakening Theological Seminary, and loves learning about the ways and heart of God. I have watched him deal with physical challenges and spiritual challenges and am impressed with his integrity and faith. He is a leader whom I believe God is going to bless. God is already using Tyler to reach millennials. He is a creative, has the heart of an evangelist, and wants to see the church of Jesus Christ grow.

It is an honor to recommend *Don't Stop* to you. In it, Tyler focuses on one theme a month, causing the devotional to be more focused than some, which I like. I believe Tyler has written a great devotional, one that will bless and encourage you as you learn more about being a disciple of Jesus Christ.

Blessings in and through him,
Randy Clark
Founder, Global Awakening

introduction

I used to think I would have to live a second-rate life because of where I came from and some of the experiences I had been through. When I stepped into sonship with Father God, I realized he designed a life for me that is the adventure of a lifetime. For the next year, I am praying for you to get in rhythm with your design and destiny. God doesn't position people for small things, and that includes you. Whether your dream is to be a mom raising world changers, an itinerant minister who sees stadiums come to know Jesus, an entrepreneur whom God uses to fund the kingdom, or a servant whom God deploys in the workforce to spread his aroma, this devotional will help you get in sync with him. Each day you will receive a bite-size piece of encouragement that is meant as fuel and to turn your thoughts toward God.

Every month centers on a unique theme, and this is by design. This approach allows us to think deeply about a specific topic over numerous days. Instead of a quick flash in a pan, these godly principles will be embedded deep in your Spirit.

I can't wait to hear the testimonies of how God uses this book to transform your thinking and your life. I am cheering you on!

Don't stop!
Tyler

january

goals

what if?

> "As for you, be strong and do not give up,
> for your work will be rewarded."
>
> 2 CHRONICLES 15:7 NIV

The start of each new year is full of what-ifs. What if I land that job I've been hoping for? What if my parents finally come to church with me? What if I finally get in shape? What if I receive that healing I'm believing God can do?

But we look back, not just forward. When we think back to the goals we set and failed at, the successes that just slipped out of our hands, they're all tied together with what-ifs.

What if I hadn't stopped?

What if I had kept going?

What if I had tried just one more time?

But what if you were just one more try away from the breakthrough you have been praying for? One more job application for that dream job. One more invitation for that loved one to come to church. One more prayer in faith to a God who hears us.

This year your what-if can turn into a wow because God has something wonderful in store for you. All you have to do is don't stop.

keep moving

Make a list—as long or as short as you want—of the things you want to accomplish this year.

past holding you back?

How precious are your thoughts about me, O God.
They cannot be numbered!

PSALM 139:17 NLT

Thinking back can motivate us to keep moving. But it can also stop us in our steps. When we think back on the past, we may be tempted to focus solely on the mistakes we've made. We look back in regret, wishing we had made this move instead of that move, that we had zigged instead of zagged. But regret will only make you feel lousy about yourself and keep you locked in your present circumstances.

Regret is a surefire way to make you think negative thoughts about yourself. You beat yourself up over silly slipups. You condemn yourself for foolish failures. But what about God? When he thinks of you, he is clear about what he sees. He doesn't see you as a disappointment. He sees you as a treasure.

Out of all the beautiful places on earth—the waterfalls, beaches, snow-covered mountains—you are his treasured possession. You are the apple of his eye. He's crazy about you! Take that as a cue to start thinking treasured thoughts about yourself.

keep moving

Keep a record of how many negative self-thoughts you have today. Now increase the number of positive self-thoughts to equal or surpass those.

dream big

"You intended to harm me, but God intended it all for good.
He brought me to this position so I could save the lives of
many people."

GENESIS 50:20 NLT

What's your biggest dream? Not a dream of instant success
or insane fame. But a dream to reach the unreachable, to
impact the hurt and dying, to change the course of the lives
of the lost.

Joseph was one of the most famous dreamers in
the Bible. From his very first dream, he was diligent about
making it a theme of his heart. He shared his dreams with
others unashamedly, but that led him to some dark places.
His very brothers threatened his life. His own flesh and
blood sold him into slavery. He was thrown into jail and
forgotten. But God did not forget. Not only did he unlock
the physical jail Joseph was in, but he unlocked the dreams
that kept Joseph's heart moving.

You might feel like you can't take one more step.
Those dreams you had are all you have, but your energy is
all used up. God can give you the strength to take another
step, and he can make it happen in a way that blesses you
and others.

keep moving

What is one dream that you've had that has failed
to materialize?

dreams don't happen overnight

They are reborn—not with a physical birth resulting from human passion or plan, but a birth that comes from God.

John 1:13 NLT

No one can make a dream come true overnight. It takes commitment and resilience to persevere when things don't go the way you want them to. The one thing that makes that possible is when you take that dream and make it the theme of your heart.

But that doesn't happen right away. You have to allow the promises of God to take root inside you. As you meditate on God's Word, passion for the things of the Lord will grow deeper inside you. Pieces of the chaos that exist in the world will begin to drift away, and your heart will be set solely on God's dream for your life.

If the theme of your heart is born from your own passions and desires, then it will never end well. You might see that dream fulfilled. You could even be successful. But you will fail at the biggest test of all: pleasing God. Instead, allow him to spark the passion within and then watch as he moves mountains to make it happen.

keep moving

Think of the differences between a God-birthed dream and one resulting from your own passion or plan.

working on your dream

"I knew you before I formed you in your mother's womb.
Before you were born I set you apart and appointed you."

JEREMIAH 1:5 NLT

What is your dream job? Not the one you think will earn you the most money but the one that will finally fulfill your heart's deepest desires. Too often we stop short of our dreams and settle for something that will get us by.

God created you specifically for a singular purpose. Part of that purpose is in what you do with the majority of your time: your jobs. What if you felt that fit every day while at work?

God also created us with intentionality. He knew what he was doing when he gave you those abilities you have, those dreams you've pondered, and those goals you've longed to reach. And if he has put them in you, then he would love to see them come out of you.

keep moving

What's the biggest dream you've ever had? How would your life be different if you could accomplish it?

don't let it stop you

Let's not get tired of doing what is good. At just the right time we will reap a harvest of blessing if we don't give up.

GALATIANS 6:9 NLT

What's keeping you from being everything you ever thought you could be? Each new year, millions of people make New Year's resolutions. Few of them actually keep their resolutions all year long. In fact, the majority fail within the first month.

Is it that they just don't want it strongly enough? Is it that they weren't really committed to begin with? It's hard to say. What is true is that the only way to fulfill that resolution is to keep going. To not stop. To remove every obstacle in your path.

In God, you have every obstacle removed. When you put your full trust in his Son, he removed every sin in your life. The condemnation was over, the judgment removed, the power of sin snapped in half. Now, it's up to us to walk that out in our lives, to take what he has given us and move forward. When you take the dream he has firmly planted in your heart and keep taking steps to see it through, you are a living example of the power of salvation.

keep moving

What was the biggest hurdle to fulfilling a goal in your life last year?

no obstacle too high

Such a large crowd of witnesses is all around us! So we must get rid of everything that slows us down, especially the sin that just won't let go. And we must be determined to run the race that is ahead of us.

HEBREWS 12:1 CEV

In Hebrews 11, we hear about the Hall of Faith. The author laid down name after name, each one a highlight reel of faithfulness to the Lord. Together they are examples of what it means to have a don't-stop attitude. But more than that, they are human beings with struggles and failures just like you and me.

I think that's why I like that chapter so much. The people listed didn't put on a mask and pretend to be perfect. They just kept putting one foot in front of the other.

It's no surprise that the next chapter opens the way it does. We read about the many fans cheering us on to our destiny. And that crowd is filled with those Hall of Faith members. They know that we're going to stumble and fall. But they also know the power of getting back up. It takes shaking off the shackles of sin though. When we confess our sins, we can keep on moving to what God has in store for us.

keep moving

Unconfessed sin is the number one hurdle in the lives of those who want to keep doing good. How do you deal with your sins?

dream small?

The LORD was with Joseph, so he succeeded in everything he did as he served in the home of his Egyptian master.

GENESIS 39:2 NLT

We usually dream about the big things that will happen in the future. The spotlight gets really big when you accomplish a goal, fulfill a vision, or realize a dream. But it's pretty dim when you're just going day-to-day. That can make it seem like the small things are no big deal. They are actually the most important.

The small things you do when no one is watching lead to the big things when all eyes are on you. When you think about the story of Joseph, you remember the big moments. His brothers sold him into slavery. Although he refused the advances of Potiphar's wife, he was thrown into prison. Then he interpreted Pharaoh's dream and rose to second-in-command of all Egypt. But in between, there were years and years of silently and faithfully doing the right thing. God was with him, and that's what ensured he was taken care of. Without faithfully clinging to God in the small things, he would have never accomplished the big things.

keep moving

What is a small step you can make today to remain focused on a dream God has placed in your heart?

no instant success

"At the time I have decided, my words will come true.
You can trust what I say about the future. It may take
a long time, but keep on waiting—it will happen!"

HABAKKUK 2:3 CEV

We live in a microwave society. We want everything now.
The problem is we don't have to wait for some things that
took a long time just a few years ago. Fast food and online
shopping have replaced slow-cooked meals and window-
shopping. Instant gratification is not just an option; it's an
expectation.

When it comes to the dream God has placed in your
heart, you will be disappointed if you expect it to happen all
at once. It's a matter of perspective, actually. When we see
someone else succeed, we get a glimpse of their highlight
reel. A friend can tell you in five short minutes what took
six long months to live out. Don't believe the lie that
fulfillment is quick.

Remember that God is faithful. It may seem like
your dream won't ever happen, but he's not being slow. He's
being deliberate. His timing is always best, and his answer
is always right. Why? Because he loves you and wants the
best for you.

keep moving

What is something that seemed to take forever
to happen in your life, but when you look back, it
happened at just the right time?

now versus most

"Seek first his kingdom and his righteousness,
and all these things will be given to you as well."

MATTHEW 6:33 NIV

There is a battle waging inside you for the fulfillment of a dream. It's between what you want now and what you want most. The now-most battle could determine how painful the wait is between your current circumstance and your future success.

Now is easy. It's all about making you happy no matter what. Have that extra slice of cake or buy those new shoes you don't need. Just push the button and feel good.

Most is hard. It's about letting go of comfort in the present so you will be ready in the future. It's about sacrificing and giving up. It may feel like you're losing something right now, but you will win the war for your dream in the long run.

In order to stay on course for the dream that God has placed in your heart, there will be many now-most battles. Discipline yourself to want *most* instead of *now*. Don't stop to take what's in front of you right now if it means not staying on track for what you want most.

keep moving

Make a list of things you want now and things you want most this year. What are some differences between the two?

it's worth the wait

"Wherever your treasure is,
there the desires of your heart will also be."

MATTHEW 6:21 NLT

"Well worth the wait." That's what you say after a nice sit-down meal or at the end of a beautiful wedding. It takes nine months to have a child and then another eighteen years to raise them. But seeing your son or daughter live out a meaningful life makes it all worthwhile. Or maybe you've saved up for a nice vacation, a new car, or a home of your own. Those are all things that are well worth the wait.

There are other less tangible things in life that are worth the wait. When it comes to bringing a friend or a loved one to Christ, you are patient with them and willing to take your time. Or how about a ministry that you've been praying for years about starting? How sweet it is when you finally see God put the last piece into place and you launch off on your own.

Waiting doesn't have to be grueling or burdensome. There are lots of things that happen during the wait that make it worthwhile. You will learn and grow. You will make connections and friends. You may even find that your desires have shifted to something even better.

keep moving

What is something that was worth the wait in your life?

waiting well

If we hope for what we do not see,
we eagerly wait for it with patience.

ROMANS 8:25 CSB

If you want to wait well, patience is the key. That's a lot easier said than done. Patience is the ability to put off what you want now, no matter what. The problem is that patience can only be learned "on the job." There's nothing you can do to gain patience without actually experiencing a time of waiting.

Impatience has ruined many a dinner, a day, or even a dream. You can lose your cool while waiting for a table. You can blow your top because someone stood you up. Or your dream could slip through your fingers because you jumped the gun too quickly.

On the other hand, patience is a fruit of the Spirit. It's something that is birthed by the Holy Spirit in the moment of waiting. He can show up and slow you down, give you perspective, and keep you on the right track. Patience isn't about stopping altogether; it's about staying true to the path God laid out for you.

keep moving

What is a small way you can practice patience today?

known for

"His master replied, 'Well done, good and faithful servant! You have been faithful with a few things; I will put you in charge of many things. Come and share your master's happiness!'"

MATTHEW 25:21 NIV

There is one question no one really wants to think about. But anyone who asks it could very likely unlock the secret to fueling their life journey. Want to know what it is? Okay, here it is: At your funeral, what do you want them to remember you for?

That's a tough question not only because it makes you think about your own death. But also because it's a pretty big one. It's like trying to wrap your entire life up in one sentence, one phrase even. But if you can manage to answer it accurately, you will take a huge step forward toward the dream God has placed in your heart.

Don't answer it right away. It may take you some time, maybe a few days or weeks, to come up with the right answer. But when you do, you will have the theme of your life. The one thing you want more than anything else. The desire that rises to the top.

keep moving

Start answering that question by thinking of just one thing, big or small, that you want to be remembered for.

keep your eyes on the prize

We must keep our eyes on Jesus,
who leads us and makes our faith complete.

HEBREWS 12:2 CEV

Running isn't for everyone. But those who do enjoy
running use a few techniques to keep themselves focused
on finishing a race. One of those is to take the very next
step. Just one more step. One foot after the other. Don't
count how many yards, meters, or miles you have left.

Another thing runners do is to set their eyes on the
finish line. Don't look from side to side.

It is vital to refocus your perspective so you can
continue to operate toward the dream or the position of
influence God has for you. Without perspective, you will
lose steam—fast! You may often feel tired during your quest
for fulfillment not because the path is too hard but because
you've shifted your focus from what's most important.

Often in life our perspectives shift. Over time,
it's easy to get off track. We may get complacent or
feel overwhelmed. We can get sidetracked by other
opportunities that are good but just aren't for us.

Continually keep your eyes on Jesus, knowing that
he will never lead you off course.

keep moving

What are some ways that your perspective has shifted
from your goal and to things that don't matter?

what's your contribution?

He makes the whole body fit together perfectly.
As each part does its own special work,
it helps the other parts grow, so that the whole body
is healthy and growing and full of love.

EPHESIANS 4:16 NLT

On the ball field, at work, and even at home, we all contribute something. A good worker will contribute to the bottom line. A good stay-at-home parent will contribute to the housework. A good teammate will contribute to the winning goal. A good student contributes in class.

We all want to make a contribution to the world around us. Some of us dream of big contributions, like leading a large organization or being at the head of a movement. Others think of small contributions, like brightening someone's day or helping a neighbor in need.

The truth is that we can all make large and small contributions in the world. And we should! God has empowered you not only to move mountains but also to love your neighbor. In fact, the largest contribution you can make will actually be the result of continued faithful contributions along the way. What do you think you can do? How best can God use your skills and talents and desires and passions? Who will receive your contributions?

keep moving

What small act of kindness can you do today to
contribute to someone else's life?

advice you can take

Fools think they know what is best,
but a sensible person listens to advice.

PROVERBS 12:15 CEV

Where do you go for the best advice? A trusted friend? A professional? The internet? There are so many places for us to look for advice, but the best advice when it comes to fulfilling the dream God has placed in your heart is found at the source—God himself. His Word has given us all we need for living a godly life.

But what happens when we don't like the advice we hear? Our natural response is to find an escape or an excuse. We try to find a loophole, a way out. Maybe we tell ourselves that the Bible doesn't really say what it says or that it doesn't really apply to us and our life.

The wise listen to advice and take it. When we know that God has his best lined up for us, we can trust him at his word. We can take his advice and move forward, knowing that we will succeed. There is no better source for great advice than God himself. So don't be afraid to follow through on what he has told you to do.

keep moving

What is one thing you know you should be doing but you've been putting off?

easier said than done

Dear brothers and sisters, when troubles of any kind come your way, consider it an opportunity for great joy.

JAMES 1:2 NLT

"That's easy for you to say."

It's a phrase we have on hand whenever we hear good advice we don't want to take. Maybe we think that whoever is giving us that advice hasn't gone through what we have. Or perhaps we think our condition is just so much worse than others can believe.

But what happens when that advice comes from the Bible? Paul told us in Romans 5:3 that we can rejoice when we run into trials and troubles. The advice we want to hear is that we can get overwhelmed when we run into trials or we can just give up when we face troubles. Instead, he declared that any trial or trouble is a cause for joy.

That's easy for him to say, right? Well, not really. If you read through his life story, you'll find plenty of times when he suffered trials and troubles. He was thrown into jail, beaten, left for dead, shipwrecked, starved, and ultimately killed. But he faced it all with joy. Romans 5:3 offers some tough advice to take, but when you consider the source, you realize it's also great advice.

keep moving

What is one bad thing that's happened to you that could cause you to rejoice?

sole source of joy and life

To me to live is Christ,
and to die is gain.

PHILIPPIANS 1:21 ESV

Nothing can hold you back. Nothing can stop you. There is no struggle in life that can get you down. As long as you focus on the most important thing.

Paul had the right to tell us to rejoice in our struggles because he lived through his own suffering. What was the difference? He refused to make his struggles the center of his life. Instead, he put Jesus in the center and let everything revolve around Jesus.

When we make Jesus the sole source of our joy and life, we can view anything through the lens of Christ's love for us. This is how we shift our perspective. When we face struggles, we view them through the scope of Jesus' promises for our lives. When we have success, we peek at it through the eyes of generosity he has given us. When we suffer a setback, we read it through the truth of his revealed Word. How you look at the world will be determined by who you put in the center of it.

keep moving

What is your first response when you face a struggle in life? Do you think that response is helpful or hurtful?

the roots of our struggles

I may walk through valleys as dark as death, but I won't be afraid. You are with me, and your shepherd's rod makes me feel safe.

PSALM 23:4 CEV

Be honest with yourself. What's got you stuck in life? What is holding you back? What is hanging off you that, if you shook it off, you just know you'd be able to move forward?

It may be a circumstance, something outside your control. Something bad happened to you, or worse, someone did something bad to you. You were hurt, wounded, damaged. You've been left broken, weak, scarred. And now you feel powerless to move forward. You're stuck.

These are the roots of our struggles. The first step in getting past them is to identify them. That's where you need to begin. But remember, no matter what that struggle is, it's never too big to stop you if you have God on your side. He has promised to never leave you or forsake you. When you are brokenhearted, he is close to you. When you mess up, he's there to pick you up. And he is your biggest cheerleader, waiting to see the smile on your face as you finish the race.

keep moving

What is your biggest struggle in life?

the struggle is real

The righteous person faces many troubles,
but the LORD comes to the rescue each time.

PSALM 34:19 NLT

Have you ever heard the phrase "The struggle is real"?
We usually use it sarcastically to describe some minor
inconvenience. Maybe they forgot the ketchup with your
drive-through order. Or it's raining on your day off. These
aren't real struggles in life even if they can be the straw that
breaks the camel's back.

The real struggles in life are the big things that come
out of nowhere, wreak havoc, and then move on. We're left
with a mess we have to clean up. Our car breaks down. We
get laid off. A relative is in the hospital. All in the same week!

These are real struggles. And the worst thing we can
do is ignore them. Pretending that your life is perfect won't
make it that way. Instead, be honest about your struggle
and hopeful in the Lord. Yes, there are real struggles. But
there is a stronger God who loves you and holds the future
in his hands.

keep moving

Practice telling yourself that your God is bigger than
your struggles today.

the good also struggle

Friends, when life gets really difficult, don't jump to
the conclusion that God isn't on the job. Instead,
be glad that you are in the very thick of what Christ
experienced. This is a spiritual refining process,
with glory just around the corner.

1 PETER 4:12–13 MSG

We all struggle with things in our lives. Some of us struggle
with our schedule, always late for appointments. Others
struggle with technology. Many of us struggle with self-
image, either having an overinflated ego or constant self-
doubt. And all of us struggle with sin.

It's true that we should avoid sin at all costs. Not only
does it erode our relationship with the Lord, but it can also
cause massive destruction in our personal lives. When we
hear that someone is struggling with sin, we think that they
are losing the battle. But that's not always true.

We need to reframe how we talk about struggling
with sin. Struggling with something does not mean you
are not successful. In fact, anyone who has succeeded in
life will tell you about the daily struggles they face. The
opposite of struggling is giving up. If you struggle with sin,
keep struggling! Don't give up, and don't give in. It's only
through struggle that you will overcome and be victorious.

keep moving

Name one sin you struggle with over and over again,
and then name three strategies to battle against that sin.

life unfiltered

Christ has taken hold of me. So I keep on running
and struggling to take hold of the prize.

PHILIPPIANS 3:12 CEV

One of the most amazing technological advances in the past twenty years may just be the Instagram filter. You can take an average photograph and turn it into a work of art with one click. You can change how you look and what others think about you too. But the filter also sets the bar way too high. All social media is cluttered with unrealistic images of perfection and beauty that none of us can live up to.

I'm convinced that Paul would have never used a filter if social media were around in his day. Why do I say that? Because his letters are full of unfiltered truth. Not just the truth he shared about God but the truth about himself as well. Instead of giving the impression that he was perfect, he talked openly of his past life of sin and his present struggles. He never let on that everything was going better than it really was. What he did was amplify his own weaknesses because he knew that God was his true strength. It's refreshing to see that such a pioneer of the faith had his own struggles. His openness and his unfiltered life challenge us to also be unfiltered in our trust of God's strength.

keep moving

What is one unfiltered statement you could make
about your own life?

stop watching the highlight reel

If I must boast, I would rather boast about the things that show how weak I am.

2 CORINTHIANS 11:30 NLT

Social media will often distort reality. We are shown other people's highlight reels while being reminded of the lows we are living through. It's rare for people to share their struggles online, and when they do, they usually share it in a way that makes themselves look better.

Paul shared both his ups and downs throughout his life. Philippians 4:12 tells us that he had lived with a lot of privilege but also with nothing at all. In 2 Corinthians 11:23–27, he shared plenty of times when his life was turned upside down. That list includes imprisonment, beatings, lashings, and stonings. He talked about shipwrecks and near-death escapes. But through it all, he relied on God's power to get him out.

What amazing trust! It's one thing to be motivated by someone else's success story. But a struggle story may be even more inspiring. Knowing that someone can be dealt such harsh circumstances and still make it through should shine a light on our present struggles and give us hope for a bright tomorrow.

keep moving

How do you share your struggles and successes with others, whether online or in person?

don't forget about me

I trust in your unfailing love.
I will rejoice because you have rescued me.

PSALM 13:5 NLT

Have you ever felt forgotten? Maybe you feel that God promised you something, but it hasn't happened yet. It can get you down and make you want to stop. But even the godliest men and women of Scripture felt the same as you.

King David was a man of courage and wisdom. God chose him at a young age because the Lord saw something in him. And at the height of his early success, after slaying the giant Goliath, he actually faced his biggest struggle. Abandoned by his countrymen and pursued by the king, he was forced into hiding.

In that moment of struggle, David sat down and wrote a song of praise to God. Psalm 13 opens with an acknowledgment of his feelings. Had God abandoned him forever? Would he always be struggling and suffering? How long would this go on?

But it ends on a note of hope. David was facing death daily, but he awakened each morning with renewed power because of God's faithfulness to him. No matter what you are facing each day, know that God has not forgotten you.

keep moving

Do you ever feel that God has forgotten you? What do you do in those moments?

worst-case scenario

Do not be anxious about anything, but in every situation, by prayer and petition, with thanksgiving, present your requests to God.

PHILIPPIANS 4:6 NIV

What's the worst that could happen? Before you answer that, think about this. The worst rarely ever happens. But when we think of the worst-possible scenario, it immediately puts our body, our mind, and even our soul in a state of fight or flight. We get nervous and tense. Our blood pressure rises. Our spirit starts to weigh heavily.

Some of us actually live our lives expecting the worst to happen. We see a check engine light and think that our car is going to fall apart at any second. We get a call from our kid's school and brace for bad news. What we fail to do in those situations is believe God's best for our lives.

What happens when we view life through the lens of a worst-case scenario? We think that every small problem is a big hurdle. We believe that every little mess is a huge mistake. Instead of living life expecting the worst, let's lean into God's provision and hope for the best.

keep moving

Think of a time when you anticipated a worst-case scenario but it didn't happen. Was it worth the worry?

never saw it coming

I pray that God, the source of hope, will fill you completely with joy and peace because you trust in him. Then you will overflow with confident hope through the power of the Holy Spirit.

ROMANS 15:13 NLT

Have you ever said, "I didn't see that coming"? In those situations, struggles seem to be magnified. Getting blindsided in life will leave you reeling. But what's often worse are the rash decisions we make in the moment.

Think about what happens when a struggle hits you out of nowhere. You go from seeing clearly to seeing cloudy. You start to lose sight of God's promises and provisions. And then you lose hope. I don't mention this to guilt you. It's our honest human response to problems we didn't see coming. But the results can be dangerous to our faith.

The best thing we can do when an unforeseen struggle comes is to stop and take a breath. Pray for some clarity before deciding any next steps. And then keep moving forward. Regaining our hope in Jesus after a particularly devastating situation can mean the difference between giving up and going forward.

keep moving

When was the last time you were hit with something that you didn't see coming? What was your automatic response?

seeking growth

Seek the LORD and his strength;
seek his presence continually!

1 CHRONICLES 16:11 ESV

Often what was meant to cause you trouble, pain, and failure can actually lead you to success, hope, and glory. Without the lessons of failure, many businesses would never grow. Without the discomfort after a workout, you really can't get into shape. This is true when it comes to your dreams as well. God has his best lined up for you, but it will take endurance on your part.

God never intends for your struggles to take away your hope. In fact, the opposite is true. Struggles can build endurance as long as you maintain hope in God.

God can use your struggles to instill courage and power in you to get you not only through this struggle but also through the next one and on and on. Struggles can build your faith when you realize God is working through you for success. But when we think it's all on our shoulders, we might lose hope. Let's let struggles be an indicator that we need to hand control off to God, who has the world in the palms of his hands.

keep moving

Think of a time when you grew in the midst of difficulty.

God won't stop

My God will supply all your needs according to his riches in glory in Christ Jesus.

PHILIPPIANS 4:19 CSB

Why shouldn't you stop? Because God hasn't. That's a pretty good reason. God has never given up on you or your dreams. You shouldn't either.

The struggle you face can never stop the vision God gave you. He will use every situation, circumstance, discomfort, pain, or sidetrack to renew you. He can energize you when you feel drained. He can give you hope when you feel depressed. He can put you back on course when you get knocked down.

God is even more invested in your future than you are. He gave his only Son to die for you so that you would have a secure future with him in heaven. He gave you the Holy Spirit to lead you into all truth, including the truth about the dream he placed in your heart. And he will give you all that you need according to his riches in glory. He has unlimited resources to make it come true, so why should you give up when you have God on your side?

keep moving

What is something that you've been struggling to do on your own but that you should hand over to God?

strength in a shipwreck

"Take courage! For I believe God.
It will be just as he said."

ACTS 27:25 NLT

At Paul's darkest, when he was shipwrecked in Acts 27, he found strength in the struggle. It's obvious that he was scared and maybe a bit worried. But he allowed God's peace to overwhelm him when his circumstances could have. He clung to God's Word to make it through.

What did God's Word do for Paul? First of all, it came right on time. When things were at their worst, God showed his best. Next, it cast out fear. Paul told his companions to take courage because he knew who was in control. Finally, God's Word created a way out. God, in his wisdom, used Paul to come up with a plan for survival. It wasn't the easiest plan. It still took effort. But it was a way out.

God does not intend for your struggle to shipwreck you. By God's Word you can overcome any and all obstacles and keep moving forward in the dream God has placed in your heart.

keep moving

How do you apply God's Word daily to handle your struggles?

not the end

"I know the plans I have for you," declares the Lord,
"plans to prosper you and not to harm you,
plans to give you hope and a future."

JEREMIAH 29:11 NIV

Your struggle is never intended to be the end of your story. In many ways, it's just the beginning. It also won't be the last struggle you ever face. But it can be the beginning of a bold, new faith in God's provision and promises.

Struggles can stop us. We hit a roadblock and take a step back to assess the damage or find a way around. But in that moment, we are tempted to just give up. Throw our hands up in defeat. Stop believing God's best for our lives. Only when we do that will the struggle stop us.

A lot of times we expect God's way to be smooth sailing. No problems at all. But the truth is that it's often full of twists and turns. In some ways, that's more enjoyable. Taking the back roads that wind through hills can be an exciting journey but only if you take the time to appreciate it. In our lives, it's hard to grasp the idea that struggles will bring joy. But when we trust in God's provision, we can relax knowing that it's not the end of the road when we hit a bump.

keep moving

Think of a time when you thought you would give up.
What made you keep going?

God shows up

"When you go through deep waters, I will be with you.
When you go through rivers of difficulty, you will not drown.
When you walk through the fire of oppression, you will not
be burned up; the flames will not consume you."

ISAIAH 43:2 NLT

You can keep moving in the middle of your struggles.
They don't have to be a stop sign, even if they are a detour.
God loves you enough to let you continue through your
struggles. They make you stronger, they increase your
strength, and they define your hope. If we look at every
struggle like it's the end, it just may be. We can stop dead in
our tracks if we want to. But when we rejoice in the face of
our struggles, they will lead us on to the next victory.

It's all in how you view your situation and
circumstances. It takes zeroing in on God in the midst
of your struggle. Consistently training your ear to his
Word will keep you afloat. And as you lean on the rest he
provides, it will keep you moving.

As you think about the struggles you've already faced
in life, instead of looking at the damage they may have
caused, choose to focus on the strength they have brought.
Find the anchor of hope you have in the Lord and continue
taking one more step.

keep moving

Think of a time when God showed up in the midst of
your struggle.

february

God's love

love where you live

God is love. When we take up permanent residence in a life
of love, we live in God and God lives in us.

1 JOHN 4:17–18 MSG

Do you love where you live? Maybe you've heard the
phrase "It's a nice place to visit, but I wouldn't want to
live there." It could be that this saying describes your
hometown. Or maybe you have your dream house in the
best neighborhood around.

What if you lived in God's love? What if your home
was where you felt cared for and taken care of? That's what
the Bible says about God. If God is love and we reside in
God's presence, we live in love. We experience the true love
of God daily. That includes knowing the love that drives us
to keep going.

When you get home every night, you probably have
your favorite spot to curl up in. Knowing that comfort is
waiting for you at the end of the day helps you continue
working and finish strong. And then, when you finally get
to rest, you realize it's all worth it. That's the way we should
view God's love. Curling up in his presence gives us all we
need to keep putting one foot in front of the other.

keep moving

Have you ever experienced God's love so tangibly
that it actually made you weep, shout for joy, or get
goose bumps?

a love like no other

God showed his great love for us by sending Christ to die
for us while we were still sinners.

ROMANS 5:8 NLT

What would you do for a friend? Probably a lot. You might
help them move, which means spending your weekend
getting achy muscles. Or you might pick them up from the
airport, which can literally take hours out of your day. But
would you die for them? Maybe.

What about an enemy? How far would you go to
help them out? It's probably not far at all, to be honest.
But God went as far as he needed to for us while we were
sinners and far from him. While we declared ourselves
enemies, he declared his love to us.

Dying for someone else is the highest form of love.
Whether that means taking a bullet for someone or risking
your own health to provide an organ for a transplant, when
you lay down your life, you are expressing your great love.
That's what God did. He sent Jesus to die for our sins.
No one took his life from him; he laid it down himself.
And because he laid down his own life, we can rise up in
gratitude and keep going for him.

keep moving

What motivates you to love someone else?

a love supreme

He passed in front of Moses, proclaiming, "The Lord, the Lord, the compassionate and gracious God, slow to anger, abounding in love and faithfulness."

Exodus 34:6 niv

Moses was stuck. He wanted to keep moving toward the promised land, but the children of Israel had messed up. The sin in the camp was holding them all back. But Moses knew that God really loved his people, so he asked for a sign. God led Moses to a rock nearby and covered Moses' eyes as he passed. When God removed his hand, Moses looked out and saw the back of God while God declared to Moses who he was. Later, God shouted his name, a self-description of supreme love.

The "love and faithfulness" that God declared is a special word in Hebrew: *hesed*. It means that he has made a promise, and he won't break it. No matter what we've done, he is committed to us. It's in his very nature to love us supremely.

When you feel like stopping and giving up, listen to what God is saying. All throughout the Bible, he repeats his love for you. He sings his care over you. He promises his faithfulness to you. And that may just give you all the motivation you need to keep moving.

keep moving

Remind yourself throughout the day of God's love and faithfulness to you.

no room for that here

There is no room in love for fear. Well-formed love banishes
fear. Since fear is crippling, a fearful life—fear of death, fear
of judgment—is one not yet fully formed in love.

1 John 4:17–18 MSG

Once we decide to move into a life of God's love, some
things just can't go with us. First of all is hate, of course.
No one can love the Father but hate their brother or sister.
Ego is another occupant that's not allowed in the residency
of God's love. Love is giving up our sense of overinflated
worth in favor of serving others.

Another thing that has no room in a life of God's love
is fear. In fact, when we embrace God's love for us, fear will
flee. Maybe not right away, but over time as we mature, we
are less and less fearful of what has held us back in the past.

Don't get confused though. The presence of fear
is not the absence of God's love. It simply means that
an intruder is in the house. We need to activate God's
love whenever we sense fear creeping in. When you
acknowledge that God loves you supremely, any fear that
freezes you has got to go.

keep moving

What is a fear that you frequently feel? How can love
banish it from your life?

the freedom of love

My friends, you were chosen to be free. So don't use your freedom as an excuse to do anything you want. Use it as an opportunity to serve each other with love.

GALATIANS 5:13 CEV

It is by God's love that we are free. And it is by God's freedom that we can love. Fear is crippling. It locks us in place or makes us run away. Whenever we are afraid, we stop moving forward in life. And that can endanger the dream God has placed in our hearts. He knows this, and so he chose freedom for us.

The problem is that we too often take that freedom as an opportunity to do whatever we want. When fear strikes, instead of leaning into God's love, we prioritize our own freedom and do what will make us feel good in the moment. But the real love of God will always motivate us to push past our fears and into the bright future he has for us. The next time you feel fear, instead of freezing up, ask God to fill you with the love that fuels your dreams and desires.

keep moving

Think of a way that you can use freedom to love others instead of serving yourself.

unconditional

Do not remember the rebellious sins of my youth.
Remember me in the light of your unfailing love,
for you are merciful, O Lord.

PSALM 25:7 NLT

We are conditioned for conditional love. We assume that if we do something nice for someone else, they will love us for it. If we serve them, if we give them a gift, if we tell them that we love them, they will have to love us in return. We are also conditioned to receive that type of love. If someone does something for us, then we will love them. But if they stop, then we stop loving them.

But God's love doesn't work that way. His love is unconditional. I think our conditioning is what keeps us from fully experiencing his unconditional love. It feels strange and out of place. It's not how we love, so how can he love us that way?

We remember all the bad things we've done and how maybe we don't deserve his love. But God doesn't wait for us to be good. In fact, "God showed his great love for us by sending Christ to die for us while we were still sinners" (Romans 5:8). And that unconditional love can serve as motivation to get past our past and into his future for us.

keep moving

Think of a time when you received unconditional love from someone. How did it make you feel?

God is love

Love never gives up, never loses faith, is always hopeful, and endures through every circumstance.

1 CORINTHIANS 13:7 NLT

Most of us know that 1 Corinthians 13 is the Love Chapter. From start to finish, it's all about love. It tells us what love is, why it's important, and even how to show it through our lives. But have you ever thought that maybe there's another way to look at it?

If it's true that "God is love" (1 John 4:8), then what if we substituted God's name in place of *love* in 1 Corinthians 13: "God never gives up, never loses faith, is always hopeful, and endures through every circumstance." That puts a new and incredible spin on it!

When you take up residence in God's love, he is in control. He calls the shots. And what he wants you to know is that he will never give up. There is no end to his love! So let's stop putting brakes on it. We can hold on to his promises and keep going no matter what. Why? Because God is love.

keep moving

Read 1 Corinthians 13 and substitute God's name every time you see the word love.

nothing without love

What if I gave away all that I owned and let myself be burned alive? I would gain nothing, unless I loved others.

1 Corinthians 13:3 cev

Serving others is a great way to express love. It's one of the five love languages that are common to almost everyone. Any act of selfless giving is a clear sign of care and devotion. But what if the act itself is really just a way to make others think you love them without really loving them at all?

Consider this question: Does love fuel the act, or does the act fuel love? It's a question that has far-reaching implications. If our intent behind serving is purely to win over someone, to extract a favor, or to spark undeserved affection, then we must scrutinize the authenticity of that "love." True love isn't self-seeking—it's selfless. It's about empowering others, not manipulating them. This should be our first step: love, in its raw and unadulterated form.

Yet we must remember this: love and action aren't mutually exclusive—they are intricately woven together. Our faith is validated by our deeds, as is our love. Our acts of service are frequently the most profound demonstrations of our love. Love must come first.

keep moving

Has someone else ever manipulated you by saying they loved you, but they didn't?

living godly love

Love is patient and kind;
love does not envy or boast;
it is not arrogant.

1 CORINTHIANS 13:4 ESV

To live godly lives means we love like God loves. And how does he love us? With patience and kindness. Without envy or arrogance. That's so unlike us, isn't it? But it's the basis of godly love.

God's "loving-kindness," how we usually translate the Hebrew word *hesed*, is based not on what we can do for God but on what God is willing to do for us. And he is willing to be patient with us. We have no way of being perfect in this world. We will mess up and make mistakes. We will get anxious and hurry up when we need to slow down. We may also freeze up when it's time to get going. But God's love shows us nothing but patience.

When you understand that God's love is patient with you, you can start living out that patient love to others. You won't blame them for holding you back. You'll see them as a partner in fulfilling the dream God has placed in your heart.

keep moving

What is one simple way you can show patience
to someone today?

a love that lasts

Three things will last forever—faith, hope, and love—
and the greatest of these is love.

1 Corinthians 13:13 NLT

At the end of your life, what do you want to be known for? If you were to put it down as one word, maybe that word should be *love*.

The three words *faith*, *hope*, and *love* seem to show up a lot in the New Testament and even early church writings. They are sometimes called the trinity of Christian virtues. But in 1 Corinthians 13, Paul told us that love is the greatest of them all. You could make a case for any of the virtues, really. Without faith it's impossible to please God. Without hope we're not much different from those who are perishing. But there is something about love.

Love is the fuel that fires you up. It's the great motivator of your dreams. Without love, we are just going through the motions. Without love, our faith is always pointed inward. But when we hope and believe in love, we want others to experience what we have. And that's the bottom line of any great dream you want to keep chasing.

keep moving

How does love motivate you to keep going in life?

love protects

You bless the godly, O LORD;
you surround them with your shield of love.

PSALM 5:12 NLT

Do you own something very valuable? What do you do to
protect it? If it's a car or a home, you get insurance. If it's
an expensive piece of jewelry, a priceless coin, or a work of
art, you may store it in a vault. We know that what is most
valuable to us needs our protection.

God sees it the same way. What is most valuable to
him is worth protecting. He sees great worth in who you
are. He knows all about you. In fact, he knows you better
than you know yourself. And he has placed a high price on
keeping you safe.

How does he do it? By his love, of course. Sure, he
is mighty and wise. But those things are not what make up
the shield he has placed around you. As you move forward
in life, there will be dangers. There will be struggles you
face. But by God's love, you are protected, safe and sound.
Knowing that he cares so much for us, let's keep going
forward.

keep moving

What would you do to protect what you most cherish?

love rescues

Turn and come to my rescue.
Show your wonderful love and save me, Lord.

Psalm 6:4 cev

We've all been in tight jams before. They can be big or small. Your car breaks down on the side of the road. You run out of milk, and the store is closed. You are stuck in an abusive relationship. No matter what that situation is, you need rescuing.

When we call on someone for help, we are admitting that we can't do it all on our own. We are usually nervous or anxious, wondering what they will think. Will they show up on time? Will they be angry with us? But God's love is different. He makes no judgment against you for needing his hand to rescue you. That's what makes it so wonderful.

When we get stuck in life, it's usually because of some unforeseen circumstance. Before we can move forward again, we need to be rescued. We need a lift. We need a Savior. God, through his love, is always there to rescue us and put us back on track.

keep moving

What is one way you can ask for help today?

love keeps us from stumbling

The king trusts in the LORD. The unfailing love of the Most
High will keep him from stumbling.

PSALM 21:7 NLT

What if you had an Undo button for life? Make a mistake—
oops!—and you can just push the button and start over.
Like a divine reset. Unfortunately, Undo buttons don't exist
in real life. But even if they did, we would probably find
new ways of messing up.

It's not the little mistakes that are the problem
though. It's the big ones in life. Those errors or
misjudgments that lead to a broken relationship, a lost
job, or even poor health. God's love can keep you from
stumbling down the path that leads to destruction. His love
won't keep you from big or small mistakes, but it can give
you a reset in life. He cares so much for you that he wants
the very best for you. And even when you don't act in a
way that brings you the best, he can override our issues to
provide you the blessing you need to keep moving in life.
Why would you want to stop when you know that dream he
has placed in your hearts is right there?

keep moving

Think of a way that God has given you a reset in life
because he loves you.

love pursues us

Surely your goodness and love will follow me all the days of my life, and I will dwell in the house of the LORD forever.

PSALM 23:6 NIV

Older siblings will tell you that one of the annoyances of having a little brother or sister is that they follow them around everywhere. Even when the older siblings want to be alone, younger siblings are right there. If you don't have a sibling, maybe you have a pet that does the same thing. When we first read this psalm, we tend to think of God that way. He's always right there on our heels.

But the word for "follow" is actually a hunting term. It means to pursue, to track down, to overtake. In other words, God, through his great, unfailing love toward you, is pursuing you in life. When you try to slip away, he's on the hunt! He wants nothing more than to keep you on the right path, so he will hound you until he has caught you. He's not trying to take you out but to take you higher.

There is nothing better than to be pursued by the relentless love of God. It gives you assurance that no matter what, he will always take care of you.

keep moving

Think of a time when you felt God pursuing you in life.

the greatest

"Teacher, which is the greatest commandment in the Law?"
Jesus replied: "'Love the Lord your God with all your heart
and with all your soul and with all your mind.'"

MATTHEW 22:36–37 NIV

Unrequited love. It can stop a relationship dead in its
tracks. Unrequited love is when your affections are not
returned. You love someone, but they don't love you. You
tell someone you love them, show them you love them, but
they have other ideas.

God loves us unconditionally. But what happens if
we don't return that love? He doesn't stop loving us, but it
does grind the relationship to a halt. Jesus knows this, and
that's why he said that the greatest commandment of all is
to return the love that God has shown us.

Now, here's the good news. We can love him because
he first loved us. When he loves you, he empowers you to
love purely. He gives you the strength to love when it hurts.
He motivates you to love unconditionally. And the first
object of that love should be God. When you return the love
God has shown you, you can move forward freely in life.

keep moving

Have you ever loved someone, but they didn't love
you back? How did it make you feel?

how to love God

"The second [commandment] is like it:
'Love your neighbor as yourself.'"

MATTHEW 22:39 NIV

They were trying to trick Jesus. There was a debate about how many of the Old Testament laws someone had to obey to be right with God. Of the over 365 commandments, was there a way that they could skip one or two? Or if they had the obligation to obey just one commandment, which one would it be?

To answer this question was to be dragged into the debate. It would have gotten Jesus sidetracked from his mission to die for our sins. Instead, he answered with godly wisdom. The greatest commandment is to love God as he loves us. But how do we do that? How can you do something nice for God? Can you buy him something that he doesn't already own? No!

Instead, Jesus says, we show God love by loving those around us. When we do that, we are really loving God. We see in them what God sees in them. And then we express the same love God has. When you love with the greatest love, you demonstrate the immeasurable love that God has showered upon you.

keep moving

What do you do when you encounter an "unlovable" person?

difficult love

"You have heard that it was said, 'Love your friends, hate your enemies.' But now I tell you: love your enemies and pray for those who persecute you."

MATTHEW 5:43-44 GNT

Want radical movement in your life? Try some radical love.

It's easy to love our friends. It's even easier to love those who love us. There are times when we are challenged to love the unlovable or even the annoying. But what about our enemies? Those who seem to be actively against us, spreading lies or rumors about us, holding us back at every turn. It makes sense to put them in their place, right? After all, if they're keeping us from moving forward, who needs them?

Jesus shows us a different way. What if we showed them the love and care that God has shown us? Remember that he loved us when we were sinners and enemies of him. Can we do the same for our enemies? Only with the power that God's love has already given us. And when we do, we can actually win over those who have been fighting against us. We may not win the argument, but we can sure win a new friend.

keep moving

Think of someone in your life who is difficult to love. How can you show them love today?

a thousand generations

You know that the Lord your God is the only true God. So love him and obey his commands, and he will faithfully keep his agreement with you and your descendants for a thousand generations.

Deuteronomy 7:9 cev

God won't stop loving you. That's his promise. But there are other promises he's given you—like the dream he has placed in your heart—that are not unconditional. In other words, there are ways we can come up just short.

God's promise to love us is forever, to a thousand generations! And part of his love is found in his commandments. He loves us enough to share his great wisdom with us, wisdom that tells us what we should and should not do. When we obey his Word, we will find success in life. It's just natural. That's because those commandments are written in love. They are for us, not against us. They are meant to help us, not hinder us.

When you respond to God's love with your obedience, he clears the path in front of you. His wisdom will lead you onto the right track in life. It will keep you from unnecessary baggage along the way too. Obey his Word as a way to say, "I love you, God."

keep moving

What is the last thing God asked you to do? Have you done it yet?

a love that goes with you

"He will renew your life and sustain you in your old age. For your daughter-in-law, who loves you and who is better to you than seven sons, has given him birth."

RUTH 4:15 NIV

The story of Ruth is amazing! A woman named Naomi left her homeland in Israel and moved with her husband and sons to Moab. There, her sons married, but then tragedy struck. Naomi's husband died first, and then she lost her two sons. She traveled back home to Israel defeated and alone. Only Ruth, her Moabite daughter-in-law, went with her.

Then, Ruth and Boaz fell in love. Boaz was Naomi's kinsman-redeemer, a relative who could claim ownership of her property and return it to her. Not only did Naomi receive back the land she lost, but she was blessed with a grandson (who, by the way, would turn out to be King David's grandfather). Through love, Ruth turned Naomi's mourning into shouts of praise. She stuck with her mother-in-law through the end. And she was the vessel God chose to bless Naomi and the entire nation of Israel. Just think what you can accomplish if you refuse to give up on people and stick with them in love.

keep moving

Have you ever wanted to give up on someone but didn't?

love sees you

I will rejoice and be glad in your faithful love because you have seen my affliction. You know the troubles of my soul.

Psalm 31:7 csb

God sees you. He sees your struggles. He understands your troubles. He's aware of your afflictions. But he has a particular way of seeing it. He looks through the lens of his love.

Notice that the writer of this psalm said that the troubles they were going through were in their soul. It could have been that these were external struggles that caused them anguish all the way to their very heart. But it's even more likely that all the trouble they felt was internal. On the surface, no one knew. But God saw.

God sees into your very soul. He knows how you feel and what you are thinking. He knows all about the dreams you have and the disappointment you've felt when you come up short. His love is right there, shining a light into your innermost being. And he wants you to know that he is faithful and cheering you on to the very end.

keep moving

Take a moment to think about how you feel knowing that God is looking at you through the lens of his love.

hurt by love

"My close friends detest me.
Those I loved have turned against me."

JOB 19:19 NLT

Have you ever been hurt by love? Maybe it was a romantic relationship that fell flat. Perhaps it was someone who should have loved you—like a parent or a child—who turned their back on you. And we've all been hurt by our close friends. When you are hurt by someone you love, the pain is double.

Job was in a state in life where nearly everyone around him was criticizing him. But he was determined to stay true to his devotion to the Lord. He knew that his circumstances were not a result of his sin. And above all that, he knew that his God loved him. It was the love of his heavenly Father that made him realize just how disappointing the criticism of his earthly friends was.

When we compare the love of God to the love of our friends, we will find a wide gap. And that goes for the amount of love we can naturally muster up ourselves too. But be determined not to turn on a friend; instead, love them to the end.

keep moving

Have you ever been hurt by a close friend? How did you get over it?

not abandoned

We are slaves, but you have never turned your back on us.
You love us, and because of you, the kings of Persia have
helped us. It's as though you have given us new life!
You let us rebuild your temple and live safely in Judah
and Jerusalem.

Ezra 9:9 CEV

While you feel stuck—in a bad relationship, a dead-end job,
or an uncontrollable situation—you are never left stuck.
God has not turned his back on you. It took Israel over
seventy years before they found a way out of the exile, but
when they did, they were glad and rejoiced.

God showed his children he wouldn't abandon them.
He moved heaven and earth, literally rewriting history,
to bring a king to power who would look on them with
favor. And he can do the same for you. He can move any
mountain that stands between you and the dream he has
placed in your heart.

What are you waiting for? Start praising God for the
answer now! Receive his freedom and be glad that you are
no longer enslaved to being stuck.

keep moving

Think of a time when God moved behind the scenes
because he loved you.

wide, long, high, and deep

May you have the power to understand,
as all God's people should, how wide,
how long, how high, and how deep his love is.

EPHESIANS 3:18 NLT

Can you even grasp the enormous power of God's love?
We can try. But there are so many dimensions to it that it's
really unfathomable.

He loves you with a wide love—spreading his arms
out and waiting for you to run into them so he can show
you how much he cares.

He loves you with a long love—being merciful and
patient with you, overlooking your faults and forgiving
your sins.

He loves you with a high love—reaching to the
heavens and back, letting nothing stand in his way.

He loves you with a deep love—wanting nothing
more than to see you grow into a mature person able to
take on whatever comes your way.

Take these four dimensions as a sign that he wants
you to not give up. Don't stop! Because his love hasn't.

keep moving

Which of those four dimensions of God's love—wide,
long, high, and deep—means the most to you today?

can't contain

May the Lord make your love increase and overflow for
each other and for everyone else, just as ours does for you.

1 Thessalonians 3:12 niv

Have you ever eaten so much you were literally stuffed? As
if you couldn't take one more bite. You didn't mean to, but
the food was just so good that you kept eating. You were
practically miserable afterward, but it was worth it.

Now think about your heart. Imagine it being as
stuffed as your stomach, packed in on all sides with God's
love. So much that it starts to spill out! Now you're getting
the picture. This is the prayer Paul had for us, that we would
all be so full of God's love that it just pours out of us.

Maybe you've met someone like that. It seems
that they are just naturally happy. But perhaps they are
supernaturally loving. They have found the secret to being
so full of God's love they can't contain it, and they have to
share it. They keep going on and on about how great God
is and how much they love others. I think God would want
that for all of us.

keep moving

Take a moment to breathe in the love of God and ask
him to let it overflow in your heart.

what is God showing you?

Show me the wonders of your great love, you who save by
your right hand those who take refuge in you from their foes.

PSALM 17:7 NIV

"What is God telling you?" Maybe you've been asked this
question before. Or perhaps you've asked someone else. It can
be an exciting question because it gets to the heart of where
he is leading you, what dreams he has placed in your heart.

Maybe another question we can ask is, "What is God
showing you?" He will speak to you throughout the day in
different ways. There's the still, small voice within. But there
are also conversations with friends, opportunities we can
take, or even just signs in the air.

One thing he will always show you is his love. The
psalmist asked God to show off the wonders of his love, the
things that amaze and astound. The things too unbelievable
to be true. When you see how God's love is moving in
the world around you, it does something. It gives you a
new energy to keep going, to never give up. That's how
wonderful his love for you is!

keep moving

How has God shown up in your world in a way that
showed off his wonderful love?

the presence of love

I love your sanctuary, LORD,
the place where your glorious presence dwells.

PSALM 26:8 NLT

What does the word *sanctuary* mean to you? If you've been in church long enough, you might know that it's a word that describes the big room where everyone meets. Without that context, it's more likely you'll think of a castle or a safe house. I think it's both.

A sanctuary is a place you can safely retreat to. It will keep you from the struggles of life. It will shelter you against the storm. A sanctuary doesn't make the problem go away, but it does give you a rest from the situation.

A sanctuary is also where God's people live. They come together to share in that safety and to encourage each other. Finding a sanctuary—both a private one in God's presence and a corporate one with God's people—will help you reenergize and prepare for the next step. When you start to get worn down, go to that place and get picked up. It will make the rest of the journey worthwhile.

keep moving

Where do you go when you need rest?

love correction

"The people I love, I call to account—prod and correct and
guide so that they'll live at their best. Up on your feet, then!
About face! Run after God!"

REVELATION 3:19 MSG

It's never fun when someone corrects us—whether it's
because of our grammar, a mistake we made on the job, or
a wrong we've done to others. But it is worse when someone
lets the error go uncorrected though. The best way to be
corrected is lovingly by someone who cares.

God cares so much for you that he doesn't want
to see you stay in your error. He will gently nudge you at
times, and other times he will shout orders to get you to
obey. He knows how you will best respond. And when you
do, you won't see a judgmental authoritarian but a loving
parent who wants what's best for you.

If God did not care at all about you, he would not
spend time correcting you. He would allow you to stay in
your sin. When we feel conviction, we should take it as
a sign of his great love. And it should also spur us on to
action, to keep going, not to retreat or give up.

keep moving

Think of a time when God corrected you.
How did you take it?

the vastness of God's love

Your love, LORD, reaches to the heavens,
your faithfulness to the skies.

PSALM 36:5 NIV

How big do you think God's love is? No, bigger. Think bigger! You're not there yet. Keep going! Almost…almost… actually, you won't be able to comprehend it.

God's love is so vast that it fills the whole sky. We have learned that the night sky we look up on goes far beyond our atmosphere and even past our own solar system. Millions and millions of light-years across, the stars and planets spin by each night. And it should be a reminder that no matter how big our own love is, God's love is so much bigger.

There is no end to God's love, just like his mercies and kindness, which are new each morning. His love is so vast that you can spend your entire life trying to find the end of it and you'll come up short—hundreds of millions of billions of miles short. So go ahead and embrace God's love and bask in its vastness as you lean on him for the next step.

keep moving

Try to imagine how big God's love is for you today as you ponder the vastness of his universe.

march

blessings

the start of your blessing

God created human beings; he created them godlike,
reflecting God's nature. He created them male and female.
God blessed them: "Prosper! Reproduce! Fill Earth!
Take charge!"

GENESIS 1:26-28 MSG

"God bless you." The idea of blessing has gotten pretty
mundane over the years. It's such a common phrase that
we say it when we sneeze. "Too blessed to be stressed."
"Bless your heart." We throw the word around without even
thinking about it, don't we?

But what does it really mean? Maybe we should look
at the very first blessing in the Bible to see how the Word of
God prioritizes this concept. On the sixth day of creation,
God formed his crowning jewel—human beings. He made
us unlike anything else and a lot like him. And then he
blessed us. He gave us a charge to do something special and
empowered us to complete it. "Fill the earth! Take charge!"

A blessing is both a command from God and the
ability to fulfill it. That dream that he has placed in your
heart is a blessing. Not because he will accomplish it
without your input. And certainly not because you can do
it without his help. It's a sign that he wants to work hand in
hand with you to do something great.

keep moving

What natural gift, talent, or skill has God blessed
you with?

go and I will bless you

The LORD said to Abram:...I will make you into a great nation,
I will bless you, I will make your name great,
and you will be a blessing.

GENESIS 12:1-2 CSB

God's blessings come with strings attached. Maybe you
think that's unfair. Shouldn't they be like any other grace
or gift from God? But if you remember that God's blessing
includes both a command and the ability to do it, then
there must be something required on our end.

God told Abram, who would later be known as
Abraham, to leave the comfortable confines of his home
and go into the great unknown. If Abram had stayed, his
life might have been enjoyable. He would have inherited
his father's land. He would have ended up living a good life.
But it wouldn't have been a blessed life.

That life God had for him included blessings not
just on him and his offspring but on every nation of the
world as well. Ultimately, we find that blessing in Christ.
But Abram had to leave his home in order to find it. God
may be calling you to go. He might have attached a string to
your blessing that requires you to make a big move, a leap
of faith, a step in the right direction. Are you ready?

keep moving

Where is God calling you to go? How can you take
the next step today?

the blessing of rest

"In six days the LORD made the heavens, the earth, the sea,
and everything in them; but on the seventh day he rested.
That is why the LORD blessed the Sabbath day and set it
apart as holy."

EXODUS 20:11 NLT

Of the Ten Commandments, only one has a blessing
attached to it. There are promises of a good, long life when
we honor our parents. There are guarantees of unfailing
love to a thousand generations when we avoid idols. But
the only commandment to use the word *blessing* is the
command about the Sabbath.

There is a spiritual nature to Sabbath rest. Although
many Christians today observe the Sabbath on a Sunday,
the Jewish origins of Sabbath indicate Jews are to rest from
sundown Friday to sundown the next day.

The principle is more important than the practice
here. It's one in seven since *Sabbath* literally means
"seventh." One day a week, you are not to do any serious
work. You are to rest completely. You are to get ready for
what's next. We were not designed to work until we drop
and then rest up for more. We were created to have God's
presence fueling our next move. And those dreams that
he's given us will only get closer as we take committed and
consistent Sabbath rests.

keep moving

How do you rest one day each week?

believe and be blessed

"You are blessed for believing that the Lord
would keep his promise to you."

Luke 1:45 GW

All throughout history, God's hand of blessing has been evident on so many lives. One common denominator is the strong faith these believers have that God desires the best for them. There is a direct connection between what we believe and what we receive.

People are not just blessed because of a mental assent or a soul agreement with the Word of God. There is a specific belief that God is looking for—the belief that he will keep his promises. When we think of God as grudgingly giving to his children, only doing for us the bare minimum, we cannot expect him to act on behalf of our dreams. In fact, we will get from God exactly what we perceive about God.

But if you know down deep that his love for you is overflowing and his promises are never-ending, you will be surprised daily by the number of blessings he provides. Try it out! Start believing God's best for you right now. Tell yourself that he is looking out for you. Remind yourself of the times he came through. And then just wait as he throws open the storerooms of heaven to heap blessings on you.

keep moving

What is one roadblock you have for believing God
has the best in mind for you?

this for that

To all who mourn in Israel, he will give a crown of beauty for ashes, a joyous blessing instead of mourning, festive praise instead of despair. In their righteousness, they will be like great oaks that the Lord has planted for his own glory.

ISAIAH 61:3 NLT

What's the best trade you ever made? As a kid, maybe you traded cards with other kids on the playground or dessert in the lunchroom. Perhaps you're thinking of the time you traded in your car for a brand-new model. Or it could be that your entire industry depends on trading this for that. Whatever trade you're thinking of, chances are you feel like you got the better end of the bargain most of the time. In fact, most people won't make a trade unless they think it's best for them.

God wants to make a trade. He wants to take your mourning—the regrets you have about your past, your shortcomings because of a missed opportunity, the pain from sin—and trade it in for blessing. He wants to hand you a crown of beauty. He wants to make you joyous again. He wants to make you as strong as an old oak tree. Are you willing to make that trade?

keep moving

Think of one thing in your life you'd be willing to swap for God's blessing.

bless me!

When Esau heard his father's words,
he let out a loud and bitter cry.
"Oh my father, what about me? Bless me, too!" he begged.

GENESIS 27:34 NLT

How much do you value God's blessing? Would you be willing to ask repeatedly for it? Would you consider it beneath you to beg? Maybe we need to rethink the blessings of God.

In the biblical account of Jacob and Esau, their father, Isaac, was tricked into giving the blessing of the older son to the younger. When Esau, the older son, found out, he was devastated. Seeing that he might have missed out on a blessing, he pleaded for his father to bless him too. He was not too proud to beg. That's how highly he viewed this blessing.

We should put a high price tag on God's blessings. And we might do this if we understood just how powerful they are. The scope of God's blessing is infinite, not just on this planet but throughout the universe. And when we see God blessing others, it's okay to say, "What about me? Bless me too!"

keep moving

What blessing have you seen God give someone else that you would like to have too?

is anyone watching this?

How great is the goodness you have stored up for those who fear you. You lavish it on those who come to you for protection, blessing them before the watching world.

PSALM 31:19 NLT

God wants to show off. Like a proud parent who just bought a car for their kid's sweet sixteen or a wife who gushes about her loving husband, your God wants you to let the whole world know what he's done for you. For some of us, that leaves us a bit anxious. We like to keep a low profile. We don't want to attract attention. But when the world watches, God shows off. And that includes his blessings toward you.

You could say that a public component is tied into God's blessing. The first blessing God gave to Adam was to give him charge over the whole earth. Abraham's blessing was for him and the other nations. So in a way, God's blessing for you is not just for you but for the whole world.

Think about it. God is showing off, not to make you look good or to give you some type of fame but to let others know what is in store for them too. You're a kind of walking advertisement for the wonderous blessings of God. So go ahead and show it off.

keep moving

Think of a time when God blessed you and it was obvious to others.

high priest blessing

"The LORD bless you and keep you;
the LORD make his face shine on you and be gracious to you;
the LORD turn his face toward you and give you peace."

NUMBERS 6:24-26 NIV

When you think of the Old Testament laws, you probably think of rules and regulations. You think of the requirements of righteousness. But we also see guidelines for worship. Part of those guidelines is a special prayer that everyone would hear when they came to the temple. The opening line is a promise of blessing. God, through his servants, will bless you in all you do. This blessing was not limited to temple worship. That's why he says, "And keep you."

Take another look at this prayer. In Jesus Christ, every promise is yes and amen. So we can see how each of the promises from the high priestly blessing is actually found through our relationship with the Lord. First, he shines his face on us. The Bible tells us that those who saw Jesus saw the Father. In Jesus, we have the promise of God's presence face-to-face in our lives. Next, he is gracious to us. Without God's gracious gift of Jesus, we are nothing. Finally, he gives us peace. Jesus has made peace between us and the Father and with each other. These alone are enough to keep going in the pursuit of God's dream for your life.

keep moving

How can you take God's blessing with you each day?

fill my cup

LORD, you are my portion and my cup of blessing;
you hold my future.

PSALM 16:5 CSB

We often talk about God pouring out his blessings on us. No wonder the psalmist said the Lord was his cup of blessing. Not only does God pour out blessing, but he holds it as well. And he holds our future in his hands.

Imagine for just a moment that God is your travel mug. It may seem too mundane for the ruler of the universe, but give it a try. As you leave the house, get in your car, go about your day—maybe at work, with friends, or even just on a walk—that travel mug is with you no matter what. Sometimes you take it for granted. Other times it seems to be a burden, especially if your cupholder isn't big enough to hold it for you. But there are many times you are thankful to have it with you.

Now, instead of coffee, tea, or just water, think of that travel mug overflowing with God's blessings. He helps you when you feel down. He gives you wisdom when you have a decision to make. No matter where your feet take you, God is right there blessing you and helping you take one more step.

keep moving

Think of a time when God's blessing came at the most sudden, mundane time.

one right after another

From his abundance we have all received
one gracious blessing after another.

JOHN 1:16 NLT

Have you ever run out of money? Maybe you went to pay for something, and your card was rejected because it was maxed out, and you didn't have cash on you. This situation is uncomfortable, and you might feel helpless.

God's blessings are not like that. There is no end to them. You can't run out because there is another one right after this one. When you feel God blessing your life, go ahead and expect another one. It's okay. He promised it for you.

When the going gets tough in life, it's easy to start looking for one problem right after another. It should be just as natural for us to expect another blessing right after this one, to rely on God's promises and let faith fuel you through the next phase. Let's get moving because we know there's more just around the corner.

keep moving

Compare the times in your life when you felt problems happening one after the other to the times when you experienced God's blessing on repeat.

hold on for your blessing

The Lord longs to be gracious to you;
therefore He rises to show you compassion,
for the Lord is a just God.
Blessed are all who wait for Him.

ISAIAH 30:18 BSB

What's the longest you've ever waited on hold? Thirty minutes? An hour? More? It can be infuriating to be left holding the phone that long. Maybe you are determined to fix a problem or get help. Or perhaps you're waiting online to purchase tickets or get a prize. In that case, the wait seems to fly by.

When we wait on God, we can trust that he will answer us. In fact, he will bless you in the waiting. Not only does he answer, but he causes you to prosper along the way. Maybe not materially but spiritually. You will grow closer to him and closer to your goal. You will find new strength. You may even find new insights, experience new ways of ministry, or find new friends along the way. There's no telling how much God will bless you while you wait for his blessing. Waiting on God does not mean stopping. It means to keep going and learn from him as you go.

keep moving

What is one lesson you've learned through waiting?

you'll be blessed if...

Let's not get tired of doing what is good. At just the right time we will reap a harvest of blessing if we don't give up.

GALATIANS 6:9 NLT

Have you ever driven on a winding road, maybe through the mountains where you can't see ahead? You don't know what's around the bend. There could be a pothole or a long line of traffic. Or maybe you'll come out of a rocky area into a beautiful valley. There could be a long stretch of deserted highway. Or you could see an incredibly quaint town that you would love to stop and visit.

In life, there are times when the road seems to wind around corners. You're not sure what's on the horizon, but you just have to keep going to find out. If you stop, you are sure to miss out on God's blessing. But if you keep going, there's no telling how he'll bless you.

You never know what's just ahead. It may be some unknown danger, but it could also be an unexpected blessing. You won't find out unless you don't give up and keep on going.

keep moving

Name one unexpected blessing from God in your life.

before and after

You go before me and follow me.
You place your hand of blessing on my head.

PSALM 139:5 NLT

God has surrounded you with blessing. You may not believe it because you can't see it. All you have to do is ask him to show you. The Bible tells us that he goes before us and behind us. He leads the way and watches after us. He is all around, everywhere at once. And his presence brings a special blessing.

Each day you can ask him for this special blessing. Ask him to go before you, to prepare your heart for the troubles you may face or prepare your mind for people you might meet. Ask him to go behind you, to watch out for dangers you can't see or leave a good reputation wherever you go. The true test of God's hand of blessing is not in how we feel about ourselves but in how others see God shining through us.

keep moving

When have you felt God's hand of blessing on your life?

second-half blessing

The LORD blessed the last part of Job's life
even more than he had blessed the first.

JOB 42:12 GNT

The first half of Job's life was blessed. He had a loving wife, wonderful children, lots of land and crops, and God was evident in it all. After the devil tested him, Job had lost pretty much everything. All he had left was his faith in the Father. But that was enough to keep him going.

The second half of Job's life was even more blessed than the first. It seems like it should be the other way around. If you read the book of Job but miss the very last chapter, it's easy to think that he had suffered greatly but made it through. He was living day by day and barely surviving, but at least he was still alive. Instead, the message of Job is clear: God blessed him even more than before.

If you keep going, there's no telling what God has in store for you. Even if you've lost so much already or are at risk of losing more in the near future, your second half has the potential to be better than the first. Believe God for a second-half blessing.

keep moving

How has your life been more blessed recently
than in earlier years?

i want to be rich

It is the LORD's blessing that makes you wealthy.
Hard work can make you no richer.

PROVERBS 10:22 GNT

What is the true mark of success? Is it how much you own, how much you've acquired, how much you've earned in your life? Or are the true successes the things that you can't count?

This proverb speaks of material wealth first and of spiritual blessing. It reminds us that no matter what value we place on hard work, the real wealth of life can only come from God. We all know people who are rich and got ahead in life by cutting corners, stepping on others, or using sinful means. Those people may be rich by the world's standards, but they are poor by heaven's calculation. Another person may be struggling paycheck to paycheck, but they are full of God's wisdom, are a delight to be around, and are surrounded by so many godly friends. They have true wealth in life.

As you go on your journey toward the dream God has placed in your heart, you will be tempted to stop and count the things that the world counts as blessings. But God's true wealth for you is indescribable riches.

keep moving

What is one intangible blessing you have received
from God lately?

surrender to blessing

"You have obeyed me, and so you and your descendants
will be a blessing to all nations on earth."

GENESIS 22:18 CEV

Obedience is the key to unlocking untold blessings in
your life. When you obey, God moves in your life. Why?
Not because he's waiting for you to make the first move.
He has already done that by promising you a great future.
He is working in all things to make all things work out for
your best. So why is it that obedience is so essential to your
blessing? It's because when we obey, we place ourselves in
the path of blessing.

Obedience is not a test from a God who wants to
know whether we will follow him or not. God gives us rules
to obey so that we will make the right choices. Obedience
to God does not mean we blindly follow him. It means that
we lovingly abide by the path he's marked out. Everything
he asks you to obey represents the best plan for your
life, keeping you from danger and making sure that your
relationships are good and healthy. Without obedience,
we wander from this path and miss out on so much God
has for us. So as we continue, let's stay true to the path of
obedience.

keep moving

Think of a time when you disobeyed and missed out
on a blessing.

generous blessings

"Give generously to the poor, not grudgingly,
for the LORD your God will bless you in everything you do."

DEUTERONOMY 15:10 NLT

God wants to be generous with your blessings. He wants to give you so much, over and over again. So he has set it up so that you can receive a generous blessing. How do you do that? You first have to be generous to others.

God's Word promises that we will have a return on our generosity. Everything that we give will be returned to us, pressed down, shaken together, and running over. That's the blessing aspect. If you want an overflowing blessing, then be generous in how you give. Then, as he gives you what you need and more, you are free to be even more generous, and God returns that generosity in more blessing. It's like a natural cycle of giving and getting so you can give more and gain more in life. That's not some theory; it's a biblical truth. Go ahead and see how much of a blessing you can have by being a blessing to others.

keep moving

What is one way you can be generous today?

giving and receiving

"More blessings come from giving
than from receiving."

Acts 20:35 cev

God wants you to enjoy what he has given to you. He loves to see his children happy with the gifts he gives. And he doesn't shy away from giving you more. The law of blessing does not mean that we are constantly scratching around for what we need. Rather, it's that we have what we need plus more so that we can give.

This principle tells us that when we give a blessing, it's better for us than when we receive a blessing. God knows this. He loves being a blessing to his people even more than when he receives a blessing from his people. And he wants us to experience this joy as well. Whenever you receive a gift, be grateful and gracious. But when you give a gift, understand that you are gaining something even more in life than if you were the recipient.

keep moving

What was the best gift you ever gave someone?

a blessing that restores

LORD, you poured out blessings on your land!
You restored the fortunes of Israel.

PSALM 85:1 NLT

God has decided to use a certain measure when he gives blessing—a pouring out. Over and over again in the Bible you see it. He has poured out a blessing that human measure cannot contain. It's so much more than we could ever grasp or realize. It's more than we can ever use either. That's what makes God's blessings so great. He will keep pouring them out.

The reason he uses that measure is that he wants to restore to us what was lost. You may have had some dream that was stolen or a goal that was lost. God wants to restore that to you this year. He will pour out blessings to make sure you can keep moving. That's how much he loves you.

You can never outgive God. He will always have more to give than we could ever return to him. There is no way you can give more to those around you than God is able to. That's not a reason to stop short though. It should be motivation to keep moving forward in your generosity.

keep moving

Think of ways that God has poured out his blessings on you.

count on it

> "'Has anything in your fields—vine, fig tree, pomegranate, olive tree—failed to flourish? From now on you can count on a blessing.'"
>
> HAGGAI 2:18–19 MSG

The prophet Haggai ministered during a very lean time for the people of Judah. He was speaking to people who had suffered greatly. They struggled with little to no harvests. Their trees failed to produce the crops they needed. Their fields often lay barren. What they thought would get them ahead was never enough.

Maybe you feel that way in your life. No matter how much you've tried in your own strength to get ahead, to make enough, to fulfill the dream you have, you always come up short. But God's Word is the same today: count on God's blessing. He will do what you could never do. In our own strength, we are not enough. But with God's blessing, we will never come up short. The barns will always be full, the fields will always have plenty, and the trees will always be in season. How can you not get excited and want to keep on going toward all that God has in store for you?

keep moving

Think of a time when God's blessing empowered you to keep working.

a share of the blessing

I do all this for the sake of the gospel,
that I may share in its blessings.

1 CORINTHIANS 9:23 NIV

Paul, the writer of 1 Corinthians, was faithful to the gospel. It was the good news that he received from God and the good news that he shared with others. The good news was that Jesus died for our sins and rose again so that we can have peace with God. He was committed to that good news out of obedience. God had told him to share it, and he did.

In obedience, Paul knew that sharing the gospel also meant sharing in the blessing. By telling others about what God had done for him, he was receiving something he could never gain on his own. He was part of the very salvation that he saw in others. He was taking a share in the blessing.

The way we gain a share in God's blessing is by sharing God's blessing. When you become part of the process of making others' lives better, your life is better. Not just because of how God repays you for your obedience but also by how much joy you receive in the moment.

keep moving

How can you share God's blessing and good
news today?

the power of blessing

Without question, the person who has the power to give a blessing is greater than the one who is blessed.

HEBREWS 7:7 NLT

It feels great to be blessed! It's a fantastic feeling, knowing that someone loves you enough to do something special for you. And when the blessing is from God, it's even sweeter. But there is a greater feeling than that. The power to be able to bless others is far and away greater than the power of a blessing received.

When you don't stop pursuing the dream God has placed in your heart, you will begin to see that he has placed you in the path of blessing. That doesn't just mean you get a blessing from him, but it also means you get to bless others. The dream God has given you is for more than just your enjoyment and good. It's also for the good of those around you. As you keep moving in God's perfect will for your life, you will encounter others who need your help. And as you help them, you will see just how much more powerful it is to give than to receive a blessing.

keep moving

What is one reason that it is greater to give a blessing than to receive one?

hunger

"God blesses you who are hungry now,
for you will be satisfied.
God blesses you who weep now,
for in due time you will laugh."

Luke 6:21 nlt

Hunger is not just an indicator that you are missing something. It shouldn't be a sign that God has left you all alone. Instead, it's a motivator to get more of God. God promises to bless those who hunger. Not just those with an empty stomach, wallet, or heart. But also those who are never satisfied with things the way they are. They want more out of life, for good reason. God has promised each of us a life more abundant.

When you hunger for more of God, you will get what you've always wanted. Not only will he fill you, but he will also direct your desires. He will sanctify your heart so that you will crave only those things that are good and holy, righteous and healthy, blessed and helpful. He has something planned for you that only he can give. Are you hungry enough to keep asking for it?

keep moving

What are you spiritually hungry for right now?

spiritual blessing

Let us give thanks to the God and Father of our Lord Jesus Christ! For in our union with Christ he has blessed us by giving us every spiritual blessing in the heavenly world.

EPHESIANS 1:3 GNT

The heavenly world is real. It is occupied by the presence of God and the angels who are at his command. This heavenly world touches ours in very special ways. One way heaven touches our world is through a gateway of spiritual blessing. God pours out his blessings from heaven onto his people in various ways. Another way we experience spiritual blessing is through the immaterial benefits we have in Christ, such as peace of mind and joy of heart, an inner feeling of gratitude and grace toward others. All these come from the Father.

Pop quiz! How many blessings come from God's spiritual gateway? How many spiritual blessings has he promised us? The Word of God says it is "every." In other words, everything you need, everything your spirit desires, it all comes from God. And it empowers us to keep moving.

keep moving

What is one kind of spiritual blessing you've recently received from God?

just what we need

The LORD gives his people strength;
the LORD blesses his people with peace.

PSALM 29:11 CSB

It's a good practice to read through Scripture, familiarize yourself with God's words, and count your blessings. Literally. Write down different passages that promise a blessing to you. And then take a moment each day to think about them.

In this verse, God promises two very specific types of blessings. These two make up just what we need to keep going in life. First, he promises us strength. We get tired for all kinds of reasons. Often we're tired from the struggle of life, but other times we just get tired from the good, hard work we're doing. Second, he promises us peace. These two go hand in hand actually. There are times when you run out of strength and feel like you've come up short in life. But God's peace will fill in the gaps, remind you of his love for you, and reassure you that you're right where he wants you to be. That's just what we need for the journey.

keep moving

How can you use strength and peace today?

a blessing so big

"Test me in this," says the Lord Almighty, "and see if I will not throw open the floodgates of heaven and pour out so much blessing that there will not be room enough to store it."

MALACHI 3:10 NIV

You better start making room for God's blessings. He has planned so much for you. He knows that you can't contain it. His blessings for you are without number. If you started counting now, you wouldn't finish before the end of your days.

Since he's planned so much blessing for us, we need to make room for it. In the case of the dream he's placed in your heart, that means moving your borders, expanding your land, and increasing the space where that dream resides. Start thinking big! He wants to bless not only you but also everyone you come in contact with. He wants to give you so much that your current plans, goals, and dreams just aren't big enough for them. You will have to start expanding your vision. You will have to start seeing the path in front of you as a wide-open space instead of a closed-off area. No longer will you be content with small dreams. Let's go bigger!

keep moving

Just how big can you dream? What is one thing you thought was always out of reach?

blessing everyone

"Ask God to bless anyone who curses you,
and pray for everyone who is cruel to you."

LUKE 6:28 CEV

When you've thought about how your life can be a blessing to others, whom have you thought about? Maybe it's a friend or relative. Perhaps you've got a favorite person in mind. Maybe it's someone you've never met, but you have a certain affinity for them. Every time they come to mind, you smile, knowing that your life's work will mean so much to them.

Now, think about the people on the outside of that circle. Those whom maybe you would call an enemy and whom you would definitely not call a friend. There could be good reason for it too. They were cruel to you. Maybe they spread a rumor or made fun of you. Guess what? God has a blessing in store for them too. And he may just use you to bless them.

That's tough to think about admittedly. But consider how your life of blessing can change their hearts. Imagine how open and repentant they would be if you were the one who took the first step and blessed them. The two of you would go from being stuck to being on the move with God.

keep moving

Who is someone in your life you don't want to see blessed? How could you bless them?

blessing and cursing

From the same mouth come blessing and cursing.
My brothers, these things ought not to be so.

JAMES 3:10 ESV

Have you ever thought of the perfect comeback, but it was too late? Maybe you were in the car on the way home after an argument with someone, and you came up with the words that would have really struck them between the eyes. Or it could have been days later before you decided on just the right combination of insults to get back at them.

We know that we should bless those who curse us, but a lot of times we want it both ways. "Okay, I'll bless them. But first, let me get in a few shots."

God says that it shouldn't be this way. There is no room to pour out both blessing and cursing from our mouth. If you had a faucet in your house that ran pure, clean water sometimes and other times poured out poisoned filth, would you ever trust it? Of course not! And God is making sure we understand that it's the same when it comes to our mouths. We cannot go through life handing out curses and expect to also be pouring out blessing. That will only keep us stuck.

keep moving

Have you ever said something you regretted?

confident

"Blessed is the one who trusts in the LORD,
whose confidence is in him."

JEREMIAH 17:7 NIV

Life is tough even when that life is blessed. Few things in this world invite our confidence. The stock market is volatile. The news is unreliable. The weather can turn in an instant. But God's blessings are always secure.

To be confident doesn't mean to believe in yourself, to be sure of who you are. It means to confide in something, like when you confide a secret to a friend. You are sure they will not tell anyone. You are sure they will keep a promise. To be confident means we confide in God. We know that he will keep us safe and secure. He is never shifting, always constant. And we can trust him. That's part of his blessing to us. When the rest of the world is in turmoil, he is never troubled. Even when we act in ways we shouldn't, he remains faithful. He will always keep us steady no matter if we are stuck or moving strong. We can be confident in his blessing.

keep moving

Make a list of ways you can be confident in God today.

a generation blessed

Their children will be successful everywhere;
an entire generation of godly people will be blessed.

PSALM 112:2 NLT

This dream you are working toward this year is not for you, not completely anyway. You are the main actor, sure. But it's about what you will do, how you obey God's words, and how many ways he will bless you for it. But don't get shortsighted. The Bible promises that a generation behind you will be blessed.

The work you do today has the power to reverberate for years and decades and even centuries. You can influence countless others who go behind you. You will be laying the groundwork for a great blessing to be continually poured out. That's why it is so vitally important that you don't give up.

God has promised to bless you in all you do. So go do it! Don't be scared. Instead, be encouraged that this will last long after you are gone. There is no telling what the words you speak, the acts of kindness you perform, or the foundation you build today can do.

keep moving

What do you want for future generations?

endurance

Blessed is the one who endures trials, because when he has stood the test he will receive the crown of life that God has promised to those who love him.

JAMES 1:12 CSB

Who is blessed? We could make a list of those whom God blesses: the obedient, the loving, the faithful. But one group you should never leave out is those who show endurance. No matter the struggle in life, God has called us to endure. When we do that, he promises us blessings.

What kind of blessing? A crown of life. At the end of our lives, we will receive a new name and a new home. That crown signifies victory in this life over all the trials and tests that sought to keep us from moving forward. When we get stuck, we put that crown in jeopardy. But when we commit to endure and determine to put one foot in front of the other in the pursuit of the dream that God has placed in our hearts, we are putting ourselves in the winner's circle. How great will it feel to hear, "Well done, good and faithful servant"! That's just the beginning of the blessing he has planned for us if we don't stop.

keep moving

Think of a time you endured a trial.

april

resurrection power

wouldn't it be great?

"Even the Son of Man did not come to be served; he came to serve and to give his life to redeem many people."

MARK 10:45 GNT

Wouldn't it be great to be waited on hand and foot? I'm not talking about going to an all-inclusive resort for a vacation or spending a week on a cruise ship. I mean having someone who cooks all your meals, washes all your dishes, and does all your laundry, and all you have to do is sit back and relax.

The truth is that this is no way to live. The lap of luxury is fun to visit, but you wouldn't want to live there. Why? Because you would get stuck pretty quick. With no stress and no challenge, your life would be void of any goal or ambition. The dream God has placed in your heart would go nowhere because you were more concerned with your own comfort than your own growth.

Jesus could have lived this way. He had every right as the Son of God. But instead, he gave his life. He served instead of being served. Rather than have others lay down their lives, he laid his own down. That's what kept him going, and it's what will keep you going as well.

keep moving

What is one luxury you wish you had? How would it change your life?

toward the cross

Keep your eyes on Jesus, who both began and finished this race we're in. Study how he did it. Because he never lost sight of where he was headed.

HEBREWS 12:1-3 MSG

Have you ever been in a footrace? You're either at the head of the pack or behind someone. In any race, there is a pacesetter, someone who goes to the front of the line and starts moving as fast as they can. They're not always the winner, but the job of those trailing is to keep the pacesetter in sight and within reach.

In a way, Jesus is the pacesetter. It's not that we are competing with him, but we are in training, trying to match his pace. What did he do? He avoided sins in his life, the potholes that would keep him from finishing. He concentrated on what was ahead, not on what was going on beside him. He refused to listen to the critics. He kept the end in mind, even though there was pain and shame ahead. As we race toward fulfilling the dream God has placed in our hearts, Jesus is our pacesetter. He is the one who is encouraging us to keep going, to not give up, to keep from getting stuck behind the crowd. Let's run our race with that kind of abandon.

keep moving

What is one thing that has slowed you down in the past while pursuing a dream?

take up your cross

"Whoever wants to be my disciple must deny themselves
and take up their cross daily and follow me."

LUKE 9:23 NIV

Here are some things that Jesus never promised us:
notability and fame, a relaxing life, comfort and luxury,
political power, physical ease. In fact, he pretty much
promised the opposite. He told us that if we want to follow
him, it will cost nearly everything. But it would be more
than worth it. When we deny ourselves, we truly begin to
live. When we take up the cross is when we can start to run.

The cross in Jesus' day meant a lot of things. It wasn't
just a means of execution. There were strict laws against
Roman citizens being crucified. The most common groups
who received this death penalty were either slaves or
subversives, those who had no life of their own or who had
taken someone else's life. When Jesus died, he was neither
of these. But he gave up his life willingly. Instead of arguing
the case, he submitted his life.

What if we did the same? There are times when we
can justify being selfish and self-centered. We can argue for
our own well-being. But taking up the cross of Jesus means
we don't consider our own needs. Instead, we find ways to
serve others as we move through our lives.

keep moving

What is one way that you can take up your cross today?

be like Jesus

Have the same attitude that Christ Jesus had.

PHILIPPIANS 2:5 GW

In the 1990s, Gatorade ran an ad campaign called "Be like Mike." The sports beverage company asked us to be just like their spokesperson, Michael Jordan. Not by our attitude or disposition. Not by physical prowess or determination. But by drinking a beverage. Somehow that would change everything. For those of us who have never dunked a basketball, we can confirm that nothing changed.

But there is one thing you can do to change the entire trajectory of your life and the lives of others. That's to "be like Jesus." Paul told us how we do that too. It's in our attitude. We copy the life of the one who could have been served, could have been treated like a king. Instead, he chose to serve. He came down from heaven to live with us. And more, he died for us. He gave everything for our sake.

How are we supposed to copy this same attitude? That's a difficult question. In fact, it's probably a lifelong lesson. It doesn't have to mean giving your life for another, but for some that's exactly what it is. More than that, it's in how we live. By moving forward every single day toward the goal God has laid out for you, you are accomplishing this copying of Jesus' life and attitude. Are you ready?

keep moving

What is one way you can be like Jesus today?

what are you bragging about?

I am going to boast about nothing but the Cross of our
Master, Jesus Christ. Because of that Cross, I have been
crucified in relation to the world, set free from the stifling
atmosphere of pleasing others and fitting into the little
patterns that they dictate.

GALATIANS 6:14–16 MSG

It's nice to be noticed. Perhaps you have an interesting job
that others are fascinated by. You can easily brag about your
children or grandchildren. It's a little harder to boast about
your accomplishments without seeming vain.

There is one thing we can all boast in though. The
cross of Calvary. It's sort of a strange thing to be proud
of actually. It's not a bright spot in human history, on the
outside. An innocent man is wrongly accused and executed
by a corrupt government. The story should be about how
we can seek justice for this person. Instead, God calls us to
brag about it.

The cross is such a strange thing, so powerful and
yet so perplexing. It means so much because of the spiritual
victory we have. But it also separates us from the rest of the
world. In it, Jesus frees us from anything that holds us back.
The best way to brag about the cross is to keep moving.
Your life, constantly advancing toward that dream God has
placed in your heart, is evidence enough for them.

keep moving

How might you brag about Jesus today?

he did it for you

He personally carried our sins in his body on the cross so that we can be dead to sin and live for what is right. By his wounds you are healed.

1 PETER 2:24 NLT

What's the nicest thing anyone has ever done for you? Maybe it was buying you an unexpected present, speaking a kind word after the passing of a close relative, or taking you to dinner just because. There are lots of ways others show they care. But nothing can top the one thing Jesus did for you.

For just a few moments, consider the cross. The stiff wooden beams laid across bare, naked shoulders. The crown of thorns pressing down on scalp, leaving pulpy wounds. The long nails driven into hands and feet. The constant pain and anguish. The final lunge as the lungs emptied of all air. The last breath.

All that is hard to take in. But Jesus did it all for you. He bore the punishment so we wouldn't have to. He took the pain to free us from ours. He was beaten so our broken lives could be mended. And he was glad to. As you consider the cross, also consider your response. The last thing Jesus would want is for you to abandon your journey. The best way to honor him doing it all for you is to live all your life for him.

keep moving

How do you feel when you think of the cross?

victory...through death

In this way, he disarmed the spiritual rulers and authorities.
He shamed them publicly by his victory over them
on the cross.

COLOSSIANS 2:15 NLT

Imagine you're in charge of strategy for the big game.
The coach hands you the playbook, and you study each
play carefully. Finally, you hand the book back and say, "I
know exactly what we should do. Give up!" You probably
wouldn't last long in that position. But there are some times
in life when surrender is the only option if we want victory.

Maybe you automatically associate the cross with
victory. But think about telling someone this story for the
first time. They hear about a great teacher and miracle
worker who claimed to be God himself in the flesh. At the
height of his power and popularity, he was killed. He died on
a cross, no less. They might have a hard time believing you.

But now, think about how you can show them this
story. Not acting it out but living it out. By your life, you
can tell the world that there is victory in the cross. By laying
down your life for others, you can display the power of
God. Not only will you be moving forward, but you'll be
taking others on that journey too.

keep moving

Name three ways that Jesus' death on the cross
really meant victory for us.

blessed is the one

They shouted, "Blessed is the king who comes in the name of the Lord! Peace in heaven and glory to God."

LUKE 19:38 CEV

Lined up on either side of the road leading into Jerusalem, followers, onlookers, and the curious watched as Jesus rode into the city for the Passover celebration. All of a sudden, one by one, they responded by throwing bunches of palm leaves down on the ground. Imagine it starting with just one person. Then another threw a branch. Until the whole crowd was responding. Those who had doubted. Those who believed. Those who had been touched by this man. Those who had seen him for the first time.

And then they began to shout, louder and louder, a blessing to God, for that's who Jesus was. A way to signify that what was going to happen would be life-changing. Perhaps they sensed it, but more likely they had no idea. They did know that this man was the one who was blessed.

The Messiah. That's what the word means: "the blessed one." And not only is Jesus blessed, but he also blesses us. When we throw our lives down at his feet to bless him, he, in turn, picks us up to follow him. Will you choose to keep going after the Lord?

keep moving

How can your life reflect this exuberant shout of "Blessed is the king"?

do what you can

"She has done what she could and has anointed my body
for burial ahead of time."

MARK 14:8 NLT

While at Bethany the week before his crucifixion, Jesus
was eating dinner at the home of a very prominent believer
in town. At the same time, a very well-known sinner
approached him. She got down on her knees and broke
a vial of extremely expensive perfume. She poured it out
on his head and his feet. Having received not even a foot
washing from his host, Jesus made the comment that
this woman did more than any other person there could.
Somehow sensing what was to come, she had anointed him
in advance for his death and burial.

   In the Bible, a blessing is often associated with the
anointing of oil or perfume. In her own way, this woman
blessed Jesus. And in doing so, she was also blessed. In life,
it's a good thing to seek a blessing from God. He can use
that blessing to fuel your dreams and passions. When we
bless God by doing what we can, he will bless us in return.
It doesn't have to be a lot; it just has to be from our heart.

keep moving

What is one thing you can do today to bless God?

it is finished

Jesus drank the wine and said, "It is finished!"
Then he bowed his head and gave up his spirit.

JOHN 19:30 GNT

The moment had come. The last hour had finally ticked away. The hands of the clock came to rest. Jesus had breathed his last breath on earth. He had died. What was meant to be a victory for his enemies would turn out to be a major defeat for the armies of spiritual darkness. Did they know it?

On that hill outside Jerusalem, a historical scene had played out. But deeper in the spiritual depths of this world, another was just starting. When Jesus cried, "It is finished," he didn't mean that his life was over, that his mission failed, that he was giving up. Instead, he meant that the worthless pursuit of religion and self had finally ended. No longer would people live their lives without purpose or direction. Instead, a new life was just beginning to dawn. And it was all because of what Jesus did. Because he finished the work, so can we. We take up the baton that he laid down on calvary. We keep running toward the goal of life change everywhere we find it. It is finished…but it's also just begun.

keep moving

Consider the cross. How does it change the way you live today?

where are you looking?

As they were frightened and bowed their faces to the ground, the men said to them, "Why do you seek the living among the dead? He is not here, but has risen."

LUKE 24:5-6 ESV

The tomb was empty. The grave was defeated. But still Jesus' followers came looking for him. They saw the stone rolled away but looked inside anyway. Instead of finding the body of their teacher, what greeted them was an angel, a messenger of God, to inform them of the truth, the same truth Jesus had been predicting for weeks, months, even years. Why were they looking for the living among the dead?

People travel to the Holy Land every day to visit the tomb. In the last two thousand years, no one has been able to find a body there belonging to Jesus. Why? Because that tomb is the place of the dead, and Jesus is among the living. If you want to find Jesus, you won't go looking in a grave.

When it comes to your dream, don't go looking in a grave to find it. Free yourself from regret over mistakes and missed opportunities. Put away the past sins that have held you back. Instead, look to the living God to bring about the dream he has placed in your heart. Go to the living to find life-giving motivation.

keep moving

What sort of dead things have you kept going back to as you pursue your dream?

what's it to you?

Jesus answered, "If I want him to remain alive until I return, what is that to you? You must follow me."

JOHN 21:22 NIV

After Jesus' resurrection, his followers were still in a daze. They had not yet received the promise of the Holy Spirit or been commissioned to go into the whole world. Instead, Jesus took the opportunity to meet with them in private, out on open roads, and even on the shoreline over a midmorning breakfast. It was there that Peter and Jesus had a final face-to-face conversation. The Lord revealed what Peter would be doing and the price he would pay for spreading the message. Peter flinched at this, and he pointed to John and said, "What about him?" (v. 21).

Jesus replied and said, "What about him? What's it to you if he lives forever or dies by your side? All you need to do is focus on following me" (v. 22, author's paraphrase).

In the pursuit of your goals, it's inevitable that you'll see someone else succeeding where you haven't yet. You can easily take your eyes off the prize in front of you. Don't let that get to you. If anything, use other people's success as motivation. Be glad for them! And use their success as a way to keep going on your own path.

keep moving

Have you ever been jealous of someone else's dream?

seeing isn't always believing

He asked them, "Why are you afraid?
Why do you have doubts?"

LUKE 24:38 GW

You've probably heard someone say that they would believe in God if they could see him or maybe just experience a miracle once. That would do it. But think about those believers in the last chapter of Luke. They were seeing the resurrected King face-to-face. They were spending time in his very presence. And some of them still doubted. They were shocked and dismayed, frightened even. Not the response you think they would have.

Jesus was not blaming them for their doubts. He wasn't scolding them for their lack of belief. In fact, he was doing the opposite. He was inviting them to express their unbelief. What was it that was holding them up? What was it that was keeping them from moving forward? What fear had them stuck? In our lives, we will have times when we doubt God's dream for our future. We will be afraid that he won't see it to the end. We can be ashamed of that doubt and hide it. Or we can express it to God so he can empower us to move past it. It's up to us.

keep moving

Express a doubt you've had about God, his Word, or his plan for your life.

don't just stand there

"The Holy Spirit will come upon you
and give you power."

ACTS 1:8 CEV

Jesus had just ascended into heaven. After spending a little over a month with his followers after the first Easter, he had appeared to them next to an empty tomb, visited them on an open road, shown up at their prayer meeting a time or two, and even sat down for supper. This was it though. This was the last time they would see him on this side of heaven. No wonder they were stuck there, staring into the sky. Two angels appeared and asked them, "Why are you standing here?" (v. 11 NLT). Jesus had clearly told them to go back to Jerusalem to wait for the promise of the Holy Spirit and then to go into every corner of the world to tell others about him. But still they stared.

Often we are stuck in our lives because we are just so struck by the moment. It's not that God is being unclear. A lot of times he is loud and clear about what we are to do. But we can't really move at all. You could say we're in good company. When you find yourself stuck, ask yourself this question: *Why am I standing here?* If you don't have a good answer, then take it as a sign to get moving.

keep moving

What is one reason you have been stuck standing
when God has asked you to move?

it's the same

I also pray that you will understand the incredible greatness of God's power for us who believe him. This is the same mighty power that raised Christ from the dead and seated him in the place of honor at God's right hand in the heavenly realms.

EPHESIANS 1:19–20 NLT

The miracle on Easter morning was not meant for just one man. Jesus' resurrection opened the door for our resurrection. One day we will have new bodies and live with him forever. That's the promise of Easter.

But the power of the resurrection is available today. It was God's power that gave Jesus new life after death. And that same power will resurrect our bodies one day. We don't have to wait for it though. It's available right now for all who believe. Resurrection power is incredible. It's more powerful than a nuclear reaction. It can create something from nothing. The greatness of God's resurrection power is also that we can use it in our day-to-day lives. If you have a dream that you feel has died, a relationship that has grown cold, or a passion that has burned out, God is ready to breathe new life into it. He will sustain you as you continue moving forward in this life, past every struggle and toward every goal.

keep moving

What area of your life could use some resurrection power today?

all i want

All I want is to know Christ
and the power that raised him to life.
I want to suffer and die as he did.

PHILIPPIANS 3:10 CEV

What if you were told that there was only one thing you needed to make every dream, all your passions, and any desires come true? You would think that it's some hype. There's no way one thing could ever mean that much. But the Word of God tells us something different. Scripture tells us that all we need is Christ. When we rely on the power of the resurrection, we can accomplish so much. We can suffer through any struggle and suffer the right way. Making each pain and setback mean something. And when we die, we will leave behind a great legacy that has changed lives in its wake.

If that's all you need, then it should be all you want. At the center of each prayer, you can respond to the grace of God by asking him to increase our knowledge of Christ. Each time you open your Bible, look for the Lord on every page. Any act of service can be a way to come closer to the same Jesus who was raised from the dead and who wants to raise your life to a greater realm.

keep moving

What are some ways you can increase your knowledge of Christ?

it's all new

If anyone is in Christ, the new creation has come:
The old has gone, the new is here!

2 CORINTHIANS 5:17 NIV

Resurrection power is all about being made brand-new.
It's not just bringing someone back from the dead. Your
resurrection body will be completely different but still
completely you. You will no longer have those mysterious
pains, that scar from that childhood accident, or those
increasing wrinkles. Instead, you will have a new body that
will live forever.

Forever starts now. Paul told us that when we are in
Christ, the new has already started. He didn't say that the
new is on its way, that the new will show up sooner or later.
The new is here, and the new is now.

Every old thing that has held you back from fulfilling
your destiny is now gone. It can't keep you from moving
forward. The only way it can is if you let it by holding on.
So since it's all new, let go of that past. Let go of that hang-
up or habit. Let go of that hindrance. And get going into a
brand-new you.

keep moving

What is one thing you are looking forward to about
your new resurrection body?

great expectations

All praise to God, the Father of our Lord Jesus Christ. It is by his great mercy that we have been born again, because God raised Jesus Christ from the dead. Now we live with great expectation.

1 PETER 1:3 NLT

Unmet expectations can be dangerous. In a relationship, if your partner is unaware of what you want from them, you will likely miss out on a great relationship. When it comes to work, your boss will never get what they need from you without telling you the expectations. Not only that, but there are also plenty of times when others have come up just short of the expectations that you outlined for them.

With God, there is no missed expectation. He is always right there for you. In fact, the Bible says we can live in a perpetual state of great expectation and never fear missing out. The greatest expectation is that one day we will live forever with our Father in heaven. But until then, we can expect great things all along the way. Why? Because the same resurrection power of Easter is igniting your soul and setting you loose to do wonderful things for God.

keep moving

List a few expectations you have of God in your life.

his Spirit lives in you

If the Spirit of him who raised Jesus from the dead lives in you, then he who raised Christ from the dead will also bring your mortal bodies to life through his Spirit who lives in you.

ROMANS 8:11 CSB

The promise of the resurrection is for all who believe. But what exactly do we receive with that blessing? For one, we receive an eternal life with the Father. Beyond that is a promise of abundant life here and now. Each day is wonderful, not because there are no struggles but because you have someone helping you through them: the Holy Spirit.

The constant presence of God in your life is made possible by the Holy Spirit. He resides deep within your spirit. He is not there to condemn you, even though he convicts you when you go astray. He is not there to punish you, even though he will correct you when you are wrong. But he is there to empower you, to breathe new life into the dead areas, and to bring healing to past hurts and sweet joy to your sadness. And since he lives in you, there is nothing you need to do but reach out and ask for help any time you feel like giving up. If you feel stuck, turn to the Holy Spirit, who is with you all the time.

keep moving

Make a list of whatever you need from the Holy Spirit living in you.

what's in a name?

"Your name will no longer be Jacob," he said.
"It will be Israel because you have struggled with God
and with men and have prevailed."

GENESIS 32:28 CSB

Do you know the meaning of your name? Perhaps you were
given that name because of what it means. More likely, your
parents just liked the sound of it. Your name could be a
family name, something passed down from a grandparent.
But what if your name were a bad one? That's what Jacob
had to bear his whole life. His name meant "liar," "thief,"
"criminal." And his actions seemed to confirm his parents'
suspicions.

Jacob felt that name was bigger than he was. He
felt lost and out of control. His actions led to huge strife
between him and his brother. He ended up fleeing from
his family and home. Then, one day, God visited him with
some news. No longer would he be Jacob. He had a new
name to match his new identity: Israel. The name means
either "prince" or "one who struggles with God." In a way,
Jacob was both. Because Jacob never gave up on God, he
gained the prestige of royalty. What's within your reach now
that you know you don't have to give up?

keep moving

What is one thing you'd like to change about yourself?

shake it off

You were dead because of your sins and because your sinful nature was not yet cut away. Then God made you alive with Christ, for he forgave all our sins.

COLOSSIANS 2:13 NLT

Something had to die for you to live. The reality of the cross is the story of your sinful nature being cut away. The Bible says that we are crucified along with Jesus. That means that we die to our flesh, our past, and our old way of life. But then, we are risen with him. We come alive to a new life in Christ. One that has nothing to do with old, sinful ways.

We all are products both of forces within us and of circumstances outside us. To keep moving past every struggle in life, we must first ask God to remove the old way of life from inside us. Then we can shake off the past hurts, habits, and hang-ups, freeing ourselves to run toward our goal. Think of the internal and external struggles we face as weights around our neck. They hold us back. They prohibit us from gaining freedom in life that we know we can have and want to enjoy. The good news is that the cross of Calvary has unlocked those weights and set us free. It is up to us to shake them off.

keep moving

What is one thing from your past—a hurt, habit, or hang-up—that has weighed you down?

too big to handle

Saving is all his idea, and all his work. All we do is trust him enough to let him do it. It's God's gift from start to finish! We don't play the major role. If we did, we'd probably go around bragging that we'd done the whole thing!

EPHESIANS 2:7–10 MSG

There are some things in life that are just too big for you to handle all on your own. Moving that couch, replacing a roof, a medical operation. All those are nearly impossible if you try them all by yourself. We don't like to admit that something is too big for us though. But maybe you feel the sin inside you is bigger than you can handle. You keep falling to temptation. You want to change, but you can't seem to gain traction. Or maybe you feel like the problems outside you are just too much. The pressures in life are taking over, and you're filled with worry and stress.

The truth is that the internal and external struggles are too big for you to take care of on your own. But you weren't meant to. God created you so he could care for you. He is standing at the top of that ladder with his hand reaching down, wanting to help you up.

keep moving

What is one thing in life that you couldn't do on your own no matter how hard you tried?

the real problem

We do not lose heart. Though our outer self is wasting away, our inner self is being renewed day by day.

2 CORINTHIANS 4:16 ESV

There is so much you cannot see with the naked eye. When you go to the dentist, they use a powerful X-ray to look inside your very teeth to reveal any upcoming cavities. A mechanic can run a diagnostic test on your car to determine the source of that loud noise in your engine. But just by looking, you'd never know. Why? Because we are only humanly capable of seeing on the surface. Spiritually, it is God who looks at our hearts. And by grace he reveals the truth of our situation to us.

We don't have a problem with our struggles. We have a problem with our sight. What are we looking at? What are we fixing our gaze on? What are we staring at? What are we expecting to see? We can either keep our eyes set on our temporary external struggles, or we can look to the eternal hope we have in God that is expressed as Christ within us, the hope of glory. We can walk in newness of life once we get our eyes set on the right thing.

keep moving

What is one external, temporary issue that seems to keep you worried?

whose struggle is it anyway?

For this I toil, struggling with all his energy
that he powerfully works within me.

COLOSSIANS 1:29 ESV

What makes you tired? Is it a long day at work, a lengthy workout in the gym, or just the stress from day-to-day life? Being tired is not all about how much work you do or how much pressure you feel. It's based on how much energy you have at any given moment. We have a finite amount of energy, and rest and sleep are what renew it. But once that energy is depleted, our bodies tell us to stop and take a break.

But what if you had infinite power reserves? How would that change the way you view your struggles? The truth is, when it comes to chasing after the dream that God has placed in your heart, you do have an unlimited supply of power and energy. We do not struggle in life—against our sin, for our goals—with our own energy alone. Instead, we struggle with God's energy. He is working powerfully within you, miraculously more than you can imagine. It may be time to lean on his energy to get you over the last hurdle.

keep moving

Think of a time when you were completely drained
but God helped you keep going.

where were you going?

You were running the race so well.
Who has held you back from following the truth?

GALATIANS 5:7 NLT

Running is not for the faint of heart. But those who are good at it know a few things about how to run well. They even know how to get unstuck if they end up in a rut.

All of us have a place God wants to take us. Places, in fact. We will all face struggles, encounter failures, and get hit with internal and external problems. How we handle them will determine whether we keep going or stay stuck. If you think you're stuck, ask yourself this one question: *Where was I going?* If you felt like you were running well but ended up getting bogged down, try to find the path once again. Where were you planning to end up? What goal did you have in mind that you just didn't realize yet? What path were you trying to run down when your wheels found a rut and you hit a ditch? And how can you get back on track?

keep moving

Think back to the goals you set at the first of the year. Are you still on track?

more than you think

Glory belongs to God, whose power is at work in us.
By this power he can do infinitely more
than we can ask or imagine.

EPHESIANS 3:20 GW

Have you ever gone through a visualization exercise? It's
where you imagine a goal and then work backward to figure
out how to reach it. It's a great way to determine which step
is your next best step. But it can also be limiting. Without
all the information you need, you might find yourself stuck
on a future step.

That God-given goal in your life is a lot like that.
You can see an outline of what's just ahead and what's
ultimately in store. But there are several steps along the way
that are completely covered up, almost like a trail through
a winding mountain pass. There are curves that you cannot
see around. But that's just how God designed it. He wants
you to know that he has something in store for you that is
more than you can imagine or ask for. More than you think.
More than you might believe. And for that alone, it's worth
it to keep running.

keep moving

Think of a time when God answered your prayer with
something that was more than you ever imagined.

take it personally

"I no longer call you slaves, because a master doesn't confide in his slaves. Now you are my friends, since I have told you everything the Father told me."

JOHN 15:15 NLT

What if you were told that the power that sent fire from the sky and calmed a raging sea could live inside you? You might think it's some sort of magic or trickery. But it's really biblical fact. The Holy Spirit, who abides with us when we choose to follow Jesus, is there with you, personally.

It's great to serve the Lord, who is more than able to do what we ask or think. It's awesome to serve a Jesus who is mighty to save and redeem our lives. It's another thing to know a God who wants to be personal. And because of that, he has a personal stake in your life. He is willing to stand and cheer you on to the next level. In the same way you would show up for a friend running a marathon, your God is showing up for the greatest parts of your life. He wouldn't miss it for the world.

keep moving

Is there any time you felt the personal presence of God as a friend?

alive in you

When he died, he died once to break the power of sin.
But now that he lives, he lives for the glory of God.
So you also should consider yourselves to be dead to
the power of sin and alive to God through Christ Jesus.

ROMANS 6:10-11 NLT

The reason any of us can say, "I know I will make it through this situation," is only because of the power of the Holy Spirit. The reason we can believe that God has incredible, amazing, crazy places for us to go is because he will be going with us as his Spirit is alive within us. Your dream may be great, too great even for you, but there is one who is greater within you.

The presence of God makes all the difference in the world. God knew that, so that's why even after Adam and Eve disobeyed, he provided special grace to them. They forfeited their place in the garden of Eden but not their place within the grace of God. Even then, God prepared in advance a way for us all to get back to that place where we could have personal friendship with God. And no matter what you face ahead, you know that you will never do it alone. God is alive in you!

keep moving

Name two or three benefits of having a living God
dwelling within your spirit.

supersize me

In Christ all the fullness of the Deity
lives in bodily form.

COLOSSIANS 2:9 NIV

To see Jesus face-to-face is something that most of us
want. In fact, if we had access to time travel, I'm sure many
of us would want to visit first-century Israel just to get a
glimpse of him. It would probably be both amazing and
disorienting. A life-changing event, for sure. But there
would likely be missed expectations. Jesus may not look
like the picture we have of him in our head. We might even
be disillusioned by it. There were plenty of people back then
who were, after all, disillusioned by the Messiah. The truth
is that Jesus was always more than the eye could see. He was
supersize, the very fullness of God in a human body. We
need to have a supersize view of Jesus.

Another thing in our lives that desperately needs
supersizing is our prayers. We need to stop letting ourselves
think our way out of prayer. God wants you to pray big,
bold, audacious prayers. He is a God who is able, mighty,
and personally involved in your life. If the possibilities are
endless, then we need to start praying like they are.

keep moving

What is the biggest prayer you have ever prayed?

from dream to possibility

It seemed like a dream when the LORD
brought us back to the city of Zion.

PSALM 126:1 CEV

This psalm was written many years after David, after the fall of the kingdom of Israel and exile, and after the return of those exiles to the Holy Land. After over seventy years, many had given up hope that they would ever return to their home, Jerusalem. That goal seemed like a dream, so when it came true, they felt like they were still sleeping.

Dreams have a powerful effect on us. Dreams can help you reframe your situation into possibilities. When we enter into prayer with a God who truly wants to answer our prayers, our focus shifts. It moves from our situation and to our possibilities. It moves from our circumstances and to God's plan. It moves from our struggles and to our victory. It moves from our failures and to our opportunities. Prayer moves mountains, but before it does, it moves hearts. We start to shed the old, self-centered dreams and pick up new, God-focused ones. Guess which ones are bigger?

keep moving

What is one God-sized dream you have for your life?

may

spiritual growth

growing forward

Let us go forward, then, to mature teaching and leave behind us the first lessons of the Christian message.

HEBREWS 6:1 GNT

To go forward we must "grow" forward. We have to continually grow in Christ. That may begin for you with advancing beyond the elementary teachings about God, the first things you were taught when you became a believer. Even if you are a believer for just a few short days, you can be growing in every way toward becoming a mature Christian.

You will continually find yourself stuck if you do not grow. Growing means you learn about yourself, your situation, and your God. It's about figuring out the *what* behind the *why* of life. Whenever you bump up against an immovable circumstance, you may be tempted to yell out, *Why is this happening to me?* But a mature approach would be to ask, *What do you want to do in me and through me in this situation, God?* That will take real maturity beyond the ABCs of faith. There's nothing wrong with those first lessons, but if they are all you have, you may not be ready for what's next.

keep moving

What is one lesson you've learned in faith beyond the elementary principles of God?

get to know and grow

Grow in the grace and knowledge of our Lord and Savior
Jesus Christ. To him be glory both now and forever! Amen.

2 PETER 3:18 NIV

Some things you can learn from a textbook. You can complete
most math assignments if you just have the right knowledge.
If you're looking to learn a craft or fix an appliance, there is
probably an online video that will help you.

But then there are some things that you can only
learn through knowing another person. Even if you found
out all about a famous person—where they were born,
how much they've earned, what's their favorite color—you
would never walk up to them and call them by their first
name or assume you two were friends. If you got to know
them though, it would be a different story.

You cannot find the knowledge that leads to real
spiritual growth only in a book. Spiritual growth requires
deep study, sure, but it will always involve personal contact
with God, who loves you, has called you, and has given you
a dream to chase after. When you get to know him, he will
show you so many ways to grow and advance that you can't
help but get going.

keep moving

What is one thing you've learned by getting to know
God personally?

grow like Jesus

Jesus grew both in body and in wisdom,
gaining favor with God and people.

LUKE 2:52 GNT

Jesus gave his life so that you could find forgiveness for
your sins. But he lived his life so you would have an
example to follow. One of the best examples of this is a
passage from Luke that ends the narrative of Jesus' birth
and begins the story of his earthly ministry. It's one that you
might skip over, but taking a long look at it could change
the direction of your life.

Jesus did not come into this world fully formed. He
had to mature and grow, just like us. He grew physically,
just like us, making the right choices and suffering growing
pains along the way. He grew in wisdom, just like us,
learning from others and applying God's Word. He grew in
favor, with both God and people, as we should. His growth
did not mean that he was smarter than anyone else; it meant
that he was considerate toward everyone else. Because he
showed himself as a great student, he could become a great
leader. And if we follow his example, so can we.

keep moving

What is one thing you can do this year to grow in
body, in wisdom, and in favor?

flourish

The godly will flourish like palm trees and grow strong like the cedars of Lebanon. For they are transplanted to the LORD's own house. They flourish in the courts of our God.

PSALM 92:12–13 NLT

The Bible compares us to a lot of different things, like sheep, servants, and even stars in the sky. When you see people compared to trees, you should always think of growth. When trees are planted near water and a careful gardener tends to them, they produce fruit. Trees flourish when treated well.

To flourish doesn't just mean to grow up; it means to grow out. A flourishing tree will spread its limbs so that its leaves cover a greater distance. It can produce a lot of fruit and provide for others if it's a well-watered and carefully tended plant. When we are planted in the right place, we will flourish.

Notice that the psalmist says that we flourish because of where we are planted—in the Lord's house. When we come into God's presence, we don't come to appease him, to try to make him happy, or to follow some guidelines. We do it to receive water from him. His Holy Spirit will teach you and guide you. And you will mature beyond your years. That's what real flourishing looks like.

keep moving

What is something you can get from church that you can't get anywhere else?

increase my faith

The apostles said to the Lord,
"Increase our faith."

LUKE 17:5 CSB

What happens when you exercise a muscle? It gets bigger. No one is guaranteed large biceps or well-defined abs. But if you use that muscle over and over again, it won't atrophy. Atrophy is when the muscle decreases in mass to the point that it becomes useless. Too often, our inner life is moving in the direction of spiritual atrophy.

Even the apostles, the first followers of Jesus and the first founders of the church, knew this. They were not content to just sit and take notes, learn about the Scriptures, and help out now and then with ministry. They wanted to be actively involved in their own spiritual growth. They asked the Lord to increase their faith. Faith to believe. Faith to withstand temptation. Faith to go where no one else had gone. If you want to do something this year that you've never done before, it will take faith like you've never had. And to get that, you have to first start exercising the faith you already have.

keep moving

Make a list of ways you can start increasing your faith.

fill me up

For this reason, since the day we heard about you, we have not stopped praying for you. We continually ask God to fill you with the knowledge of his will through all the wisdom and understanding that the Spirit gives.

COLOSSIANS 1:9 NIV

The Bible has so many great prayers. Nearly every major faith character has penned them down into words somewhere. It's a great exercise to find them, rewrite them in your own words, and then repeat them over the course of a few days or even weeks.

You can find one such prayer in the letter of Paul to the church in Colossae. Here Paul asked the Lord to intervene in the lives of the Colossians. This prayer was a little more generic than most. He wasn't asking for a specific need, but knowing what he did ask for may motivate us to keep going in life. He prayed that they would be filled up. The filling he wanted was for them to know the will of God. Such knowledge is life-changing.

When the Colossians understood what God had for them, they would get excited and move toward a bright future. That will of the Lord came through spiritual wisdom, not through human understanding. That's why it is a part of a prayer. Only God can give us what we need to truly understand all the aspects of our life.

keep moving

Find a prayer from the Bible and pray it over a friend today.

check your blind spots

None of us can see our own errors;
deliver me, LORD, from hidden faults!

PSALM 19:12 GNT

One of the most important lessons to teach a new driver is
to check their blind spots. These are the spaces just behind
them that they cannot see, even with their mirrors. It takes
slowing down or even stopping and moving your head to
the right position to see them. We all have blind spots in life
and not just when we are driving.

Blind spots are those areas of your life that you don't
have complete knowledge of. You might think you know,
but you don't. You may think you're better at some talent
than you are. Or you may not realize just how good you are
at something. It could be a moral or a relational blind spot.

What can a blind spot do? It has the potential to
wreck your life. You might not realize what kind of moral
mess you're walking into. Or it could just freeze you in your
tracks, slow you down, or cost you time and energy on the
road ahead. Make sure to check your blind spots in life.

keep moving

What is one blind spot that caused you a problem
because you didn't see what was there?

don't believe your own lies

Stop deceiving yourselves. If you think you are wise by this world's standards, you need to become a fool to be truly wise.

1 Corinthians 3:18 NLT

Have you ever heard of a "little white lie"? It's a small deception that can actually spell big trouble. But another type of lie is just as deadly: the invisible lie. It's one that you tell, and you don't even know it's a lie. Maybe it's sharing some misinformation you haven't fully researched. Or it could be a lie you tell yourself to keep yourself deceived.

The lies you tell yourself usually come in two forms. The first is when you tell yourself something to flatter yourself. Maybe you lie about how your problems aren't that big, your diet is just fine, or your habits aren't holding you back. The other form of a lie you tell yourself is the opposite. Belittling yourself, shaming yourself, or tearing yourself down will never help you grow. It will always hold you back. When you believe that you are better than you are, you stop growing. When you believe that you are worse than you are, you stop caring. Either way, you stop. So let's stop believing the lie and start moving forward.

keep moving

What is one lie you used to tell yourself?

i can see clearly now

*The man looked around. "Yes," he said,
"I see people, but I can't see them very clearly.
They look like trees walking around."*

MARK 8:24 NLT

What a mighty miracle worker Jesus was! There are multiple stories about healing in the Bible, but this one is a favorite. A blind man received his sight but not all at once. There was this sort of in-between state where he could make out objects—people, actually—but they looked more like trees. They were not clear but fuzzy and out of focus. Then Jesus prayed again, and the man's sight was fully restored.

A lot of times in life, we identify our blind spots or find a lie we've told ourselves. That's only half the battle though. Now that we've identified the problem, we can kind of see things in a fuzzy glow. We need to take a good, long look at ourselves. Maybe you can't make out all the details right away about what is holding you back. But you can vaguely see the problem ahead. Now that you can, it's time to start clearing your spiritual sight so you can see the path ahead.

keep moving

Think about a time when you were able to see clearly
after a time of confusion.

restoring sight

> "The Spirit of the Lord is on me, because he has anointed me to proclaim good news to the poor. He has sent me to proclaim freedom for the prisoners and recovery of sight for the blind, to set the oppressed free."
>
> Luke 4:18 NIV

Jesus had a clear mission in life. He knew exactly where he was going and what he was doing. He didn't need anyone to clear the path for him, but the path was clearly marked by Scripture. One day he entered a synagogue, picked up the scroll of Isaiah, and spoke the words that would spark his ministry. At the heart of his message was the restoration of sight to the blind. Clearly he did that physically more than once in his lifetime. But he also did it daily. He encountered the spiritually blind and helped them recover their sight.

Jesus is not content to let you stay spiritually blind. He wants to restore your sight. He wants to give you clear vision, not just to live a life of holiness and health but also to live a life of meaning. To be all that you were created to be. It's part of his continuing plan, and you are in the middle of his sights.

keep moving

In what area of your life do you feel you need restoration of sight the most?

the thing about memory

If you listen to the word and don't obey,
it is like glancing at your face in a mirror.
You see yourself, walk away,
and forget what you look like.

JAMES 1:23-24 NLT

Did you know your memory can play tricks on you? You may remember things one way, but the truth is actually much different. This can produce a blind spot in our lives. Have you ever noticed how much easier it is to remember the bad things that have happened to you? That's why it's so important to remember the good as well.

We create a blind spot in our memory when we give more weight to the bad than the good that has happened to us. This is why so many psalms talk about remembering God and his good work in our lives. It's so important to think about the good over and over again. The word for this is *meditation*. It's taking a truth, the Word of God, and putting it through your mind repeatedly. That way it sticks with you. When you can recite the good words of God from the Bible with no problem, you will recount the good works of God in your life.

keep moving

What is one way you can improve your memory of God's good works in your life?

the worst way to see

Rid yourselves, then, of all evil;
no more lying or hypocrisy
or jealousy or insulting language.

1 Peter 2:1 gnt

One way that we form blind spots in our lives is by the
way we see other people. We like to put people into easily
identifiable groups. We allow a blind spot to form around
that person's individuality as we ignore certain aspects of
their character. When the group we put them in is "enemy" or
"undesirable," we perceive that person as someone whom we
don't enjoy being around. We tend to become hypocritical,
pointing out their faults while excusing our own. We're also
easily jealous about what God is doing in their lives.

This way of seeing others will only keep us stuck.
When you see someone else become successful and all
you can do is be jealous, you are no longer seeing the path
ahead for your own victory. When you see God blessing
someone else and your first response is to tear that person
down, you are no longer loving like Jesus loved. Instead of
staying stuck in this lie, shake loose with the freedom the
Holy Spirit offers and start seeing the world around you the
way he intended.

keep moving

What is a lie you believed about someone else just
because you didn't like them?

how blindness misleads us

"You say, 'I am rich; I have acquired wealth and do not need a thing.' But you do not realize that you are wretched, pitiful, poor, blind and naked."

REVELATION 3:17 NIV

Many of us believe we can fully see. We are convinced that our own point of view is the right one and maybe even the only one. We will judge everyone else based on this idea even if it's incorrect or incomplete.

The blind spots in your life work together to shape your self-image. You look at all the bad things that happened in your life and ignore God's blessings. You fill your mind with news reports that just verify your fears. Then, it starts to shape the way you see others. You believe the worst in them. You see them as either a hurdle to get over or a competitor to drag under. And then you wonder why you feel so bad all the time.

Your blind spots are killing the dream God put in your heart. Blindness to God's past blessings keeps you from hoping for his best tomorrow. It keeps you stuck in your rut with no way out. Until you clear your blind spots, you may never fully move forward.

keep moving

Take a moment to list all the good things that happened to you yesterday.

a friend indeed

A truly good friend
will openly correct you.

PROVERBS 27:5 CEV

Who has permission to tell you the hard truths in life?
Maybe you don't have someone who is that kind of friend.
Maybe you have more than one. Maybe you've never even
thought of this. A truly great friend—a best friend—is one
who always has permission to be honest. They never tell
you a white lie just to make you feel better. Instead, they
can see what you may not be able to and help you identify
and avoid those blind spots.

Without that friend in your life, you're stuck. You
may be ignoring them because the hard truth is just too
much to handle. Or perhaps they told you the truth once,
and you distanced yourself from them because you weren't
ready to hear it. Make a stand today, steady yourself for
some hard truths, and then seek out the one friend who
can help you identify those blind spots so you can move
forward in life.

keep moving

What is one question you can ask a good friend to
help you identify your blind spots?

groping in the dark

We grope like the blind along a wall, feeling our way like people without eyes. Even at brightest noontime, we stumble as though it were dark. Among the living, we are like the dead.

ISAIAH 59:10 NLT

Have you ever felt you were just tiptoeing through life, shuffling your feet so you wouldn't run into anything, barely moving ahead? Maybe it felt like you were walking in darkness, running your hand along the wall but not fully understanding where you were going. You bump from one relationship to the next. Or you knock into one job after knocking out of the one before. It's as if you don't even have eyes.

We can go through life with every sign pointing us in the right direction, but we still fail to see it. Why? Because without God, we lack true insight. We lack true power. And we lack true life. No wonder we struggle to get unstuck. We are blind to the fact that we are blind. The first step is admitting you need help. But the next step is to get going. God has a light that he is ready to shine on your path and help you take that next move.

keep moving

Think of a time when you felt completely lost in life. What steps did you take to find the path again?

who has blinded you?

They do not believe, because their minds have been kept in the dark by the evil god of this world. He keeps them from seeing the light shining on them, the light that comes from the Good News about the glory of Christ, who is the exact likeness of God.

2 Corinthians 4:4 gnt

Have you ever been to a magic show? It's both amazing and exasperating. You are left awestruck as to how the magicians did what they did. But you're also shocked because you know it's a trick. The subtle misdirection of the performers has you right where they want you, believing their lie and changing your perception.

In entertainment, it's all in good fun. But in real life, it's actually dangerous. There is a real enemy in the world, Satan, who seeks to mesmerize you and trick you into believing what he wants you to believe about yourself, about others, even about God. He has already blinded the minds of those who don't believe God. They are unable to see the glorious light of the good news. They don't understand the message about the glory of Christ. But Satan is not content with fooling the unbelievers. He wants to trick you as well. When you focus on what he wants you to see, you will end up stuck. The only way out is to identify his lies and move past them by trusting God.

keep moving

What is one way the Enemy blinds the world?

guilty as charged?

God did not send his Son into the world to condemn the
world, but to save the world through him.

JOHN 3:17 NIV

Have you ever stopped to think about the words *guilt* and
shame? You may think of guilt in the legal sense, such as
being convicted of a crime. In the moral and spiritual sense,
guilt is feeling bad for something you've done while shame
is feeling bad for who you are. Feeling guilty is actually
pretty normal. It's part of God's design to make us better.
When we do something wrong, we feel bad about it, so we
avoid doing it in the future.

The problem with guilt occurs when it goes from
conviction to condemnation. Conviction is the inner
determination not to repeat a past mistake. It's embracing
the truth and removing the blind spot. But condemnation
is giving up. When you are condemned, you are no longer
free. You are locked in a cage of guilt and kept from
moving forward. The Holy Spirit's job is to convict you,
not condemn you. Any sin you've asked forgiveness for is
removed. You no longer stand guilty. You are free to move
forward in love. This is the promise of our Father.

keep moving

Have you ever felt so guilty that you got stuck in life?

blinded by shame

Instead of your shame you will receive a double portion, and instead of disgrace you will rejoice in your inheritance. And so you will inherit a double portion in your land, and everlasting joy will be yours.

ISAIAH 61:7 NIV

Feeling guilty about what you've done is natural. But feeling shame for who you are is not what God intends. When you feel bad about some part of you, the way you look, how you walk, your lack of certain abilities—that's shame. And shame will always hold you back.

When you allow shame to lead your life, it blinds you to the reality of your identity in Christ. Once you come to him, he changes you from who you were into a new creation. Everything changes at the cross, and when we come to the cross, we enter a new process of transformation. It's a point of blessing. In fact, it's a double portion, just as he promised. For everything you feel ashamed about, God has two more blessings waiting for you. Not just to make you feel better but also to energize you to keep moving.

keep moving

What is something you have felt ashamed of in your life?

clear your blind spots

*If you look carefully into the perfect law that sets you free,
and if you do what it says and don't forget what you heard,
then God will bless you for doing it.*

JAMES 1:25 NLT

How's your vision? Do you see twenty-twenty without
glasses, or do you have a slight astigmatism? Maybe it's not
your vision that's holding you back but a dirty windshield.
When was the last time you got out and cleaned it? Without
clear vision, you will be stuck moving in slow motion.
In your life, you need to clear those blind spots to keep
moving ahead. Or else you might be stuck by unseen
obstacles, including the ones in your own heart.

If you've already made the decision to follow Jesus,
he has given you access to complete clarity. But maybe
there are still a few blind spots that you need to clear. You
may look at your past through a negative filter. You think
you know enough when you only have part of the picture.
You constantly search for the worst in others, leading with
judgment instead of grace. There is freedom available to
you; you only need to get into God's Word to find it. The
same Word that will clear those blind spots will also propel
you into the good life God has in store for you.

keep moving

What is one area of your life where you need to have
clearer vision?

you'll poke your eye out

"Why worry about a speck in your friend's eye when you have a log in your own?...First get rid of the log in your own eye; then you will see well enough to deal with the speck in your friend's eye."

MATTHEW 7:3, 5 NLT

Your blind spot doesn't just affect you, but it can affect those around you as well. Not only will a judgmental spirit distort your self-image, but it will also cause you to see others in a negative light. *Why can't they see the problem? I've gotten past this issue, so they should too. There's no reason for them to be the way they are.* These are hypocritical thoughts we might have if we suffer from having a log in our own eye.

Jesus told this parable to prove a point. The small speck in the eye of your friend is nothing compared to the huge log in your own eye. Think about when you get something very small in your eye. It may cause your eye to water or blur your vision. Even if that speck in your own eye is a small matter, it may affect the way you view the rest of the world. The point is to get rid of whatever is blurring your vision so you can see clearly to move forward.

keep moving

Think of a time when you thought you were seeing an issue clearly but didn't have the full picture.

blind leading the blind

"They are blind guides leading the blind, and if one blind person guides another, they will both fall into a ditch."

MATTHEW 15:14 NLT

What's worse than having blind spots in your life and getting stuck? It's when your blind spots cause others to get stuck too. That's what Jesus was talking about when he warned us about the blind leading the blind. They are in grave danger of running into a rut in life, getting stuck in a ditch. They risk not being able to move forward because they can't see clearly. They deceive themselves and even deceive others.

A religious, judgmental attitude can cause others to stumble in their own race. When you belittle them for not living up to the standard you've set for yourself, you can actually keep them stuck in their past. On the other hand, a lenient attitude toward sin can make others think it's okay to coast through life. Without firm conviction, we might never find a firm foothold. When it comes to leading others, a balance between conviction and condemnation will result in a pure motivation to help them along.

keep moving

Think of a time when someone else was judgmental toward you. How did it feel?

stuck in the mud

*Jeshua's clothing was filthy as he stood there before the
angel. So the angel said to the others standing there,
"Take off his filthy clothes." And turning to Jeshua he said,
"See, I have taken away your sins, and now I am giving
you these fine new clothes."*

ZECHARIAH 3:3-4 NLT

Jeshua stood condemned. The charge against him was
having soiled clothes, something that was not allowed
for the high priest who was entering the holy of holies.
There was no doubt about the evidence against him. The
judgment should have been this: he would have been found
guilty and condemned to die. Instead, God had other plans.

There are times in our lives when we are stuck in
the mud. That just makes us dirty. We get bogged down
by stress, seduced by sin, or stricken with fear. In those
moments, life seems to slam to a stop, and we can't find
traction. If you've ever tried to drive through mud, you
know the feeling. But there is a way out—through the Holy
Spirit. What causes us to get stuck in the mud is our own
shame and guilt. We feel bad for what we've done, so we end
up feeling bad about who we are. We can only see ourselves
as muddy, dirty, useless. But God sees the potential in us
and wants to give us a clean slate and a clear destiny.

keep moving

What do you do when you feel guilty?

inside out

"You hypocrites! You clean the outside of your cup and plate, while the inside is full of what you have gotten by violence and selfishness. Blind Pharisee! Clean what is inside the cup first, and then the outside will be clean too!"

MATTHEW 23:25-26 GNT

Have you ever sat down at a restaurant only to find the silverware, the glass, or even the plate they place in front of you is dirty? You might brush it off and grab another utensil. Or you might send it back or even get up and walk out. Regardless, how you view that restaurant will forever be changed.

We are all really good at putting on a show. We can learn the right way to talk, smile at the right people, and act a certain way at a certain time. Maybe we think an appearance of holiness can hide an interior of sin and shame.

Jesus has a different path. The way to clear your inner life is not by polishing your public picture. It's to lean on his forgiveness. When we walk away from the things that have held us down—namely, sin and shame—we can walk in freedom finally. It takes getting a good look at what's really going on inside though. Admit your faults, ask God to heal your pain, and move forward in confidence.

keep moving

Commit to not putting on a show spiritually today but walking in authentic faith.

don't forget forgiveness

If you don't grow, you are like someone who is nearsighted or blind, and you have forgotten that your past sins are forgiven.

2 PETER 1:9 CEV

Checking your blind spot in a car requires you to move. You move your head to look backward at the traffic behind you and gauge the road conditions. What if you checked your blind spot, saw a car was there, and then turned to face forward again…but forgot all about it? You might switch lanes right into that other driver. You could cause a wreck.

In our lives, there are plenty of times when we look back to check a blind spot. But what are we seeing? And what are we remembering? When you look to the past, you always look with clouded vision. If you forget that your past is completely covered by the blood of Jesus, you may end up blind or nearsighted, not realizing it's time to move forward. You will get stuck without any growth to show for it. Fulfilling that dream God has placed in your heart requires that kind of growth. It's a commitment to some core principles along the way. But first, look back and remember all he has done.

keep moving

Share with one person today how Jesus forgave you of your sins.

apply his promises to your life

Every one of God's promises is "Yes" in him. Therefore, through him we also say "Amen" to the glory of God.

2 CORINTHIANS 1:20 CSB

God has promised you so much. It begins with his promise to save you, to forgive your sins, to cleanse you and make you righteous. We begin to clear our blind spots when we embrace his promises in our lives. He says yes to us with a promise, and we respond with a resounding amen of our own.

What promise has he given you that you haven't seen realized yet? Keep on believing him for it. He will stand by it if you move out in it. We get stuck when we stop looking to him for his promises. Don't let your wheels keep spinning. Lean into his promises today.

keep moving

Find one or two promises from the Bible to say amen to today.

live a good life

You will show me the path that leads to life; your presence
fills me with joy and brings me pleasure forever.

PSALM 16:11 GNT

The path of life is a path of righteousness. No one has
entered a good life by way of sin. Instead, we find the path
of life—the good life—when we follow Jesus. He teaches us
over and over again that godly living has rewards and that
sinful living has consequences. When you sin, there is a
price to pay no matter what. But when you live a good life,
you are never looking over your shoulder to make sure you
aren't going to get caught.

Morality seems to be a lost art in the world today.
People are so concerned with what they are getting that
they're not worried about how they are living. We need to
see clearly that our actions have consequences. When you
commit to living a good life, you never have to worry about
bad consequences holding you back.

keep moving

What is one way you keep yourself on the path of a
good life?

get to know God better

"They will not need to teach their neighbors, nor will they need to teach their relatives, saying, 'You should know the Lord.' For everyone, from the least to the greatest, will know me already," says the Lord. "And I will forgive their wickedness, and I will never again remember their sins."

JEREMIAH 31:34 NLT

As you continue to apply God's promises to your life, the knowledge he places within you will produce more and more growth. This is what the Holy Spirit does: he helps us know God better. When we lean into the rest God has provided, it's for a purpose. That purpose is not to clean up your theology or clear up your doctrine. It's not to make you a smarter Bible reader. It's to help you know God better.

What's more important to you than knowing God? Paul said there was nothing for him except the honor of getting to know his Lord. Can you say the same thing? Or do you need to reprioritize your life so you can get to know him better?

keep moving

What is one thing you can do today to get to know God better?

show some self-control

It is better to be patient than powerful.
It is better to win control over yourself
than over whole cities.

PROVERBS 16:32 GNT

How good are you at controlling yourself? If you rely only on your own willpower, you may find yourself slipping more than you want. That's because willpower on its own is pretty poor at helping us live a good life. We need more. We need the Holy Spirit.

Godly self-control is not about being perfect. It's about perfectly following the voice of God in every decision of your life. It's about quieting the demands of the flesh. It's about ignoring the passions for sin in our human nature. When we can shut that off, we will be able to turn on the Spirit's leading. He will show us a way forward, past hidden obstacles and future mistakes. You never need to fear failure again if you are able to master the power of the Holy Spirit, whose fruit in your life is self-control.

keep moving

What is one boundary you have placed in your life to help you with self-control?

practice patience and endurance

We can rejoice, too, when we run into problems and trials, for we know that they help us develop endurance.

ROMANS 5:3 NLT

In order to move forward into the dream God has placed in our hearts, we need to first practice patience and endurance. It's easy to jump at the chance to follow the religious elite or the worldly wicked because they promise real results really fast. But they are just false starts with a sudden fall. Instead, stick to God's promises on God's time.

Are you tired of waiting? That's normal. But when you are full of the Holy Spirit, you can be patient about anything. You can endure any hardship. You can overcome any obstacle. When you clear out your blind spots, you start to see God's plan take shape. It may not happen at the rate you want it to, but God in his wisdom is working all things for your good.

keep moving

How can you develop endurance today?

grow in goodness

As we have opportunity, let us work for the good of all,
especially for those who belong to the household of faith.

GALATIANS 6:10 CSB

"Thank goodness!" It's something that often rolls right
off our tongue. We're not sure what we're saying, but
the thought is in the right place. We should be thanking
goodness because it's goodness that often keeps us on
track following God's desires. Goodness is more than just
making good decisions and living a good life. That's about
avoiding bad decisions. But at its root, goodness is the idea
that service is a way to get closer to God. When you allow
service to take root within you, your blind spots start to
melt away.

How do you serve someone? Do you automatically
want to help meet a need? Or do you need God to help
you see it that way? Serving others doesn't hold us back; it
propels us forward and others too. If you are only serving
yourself, you'll get stuck. So find a way to show some godly
goodness right now.

keep moving

Be on the lookout for a way to serve others
throughout your day.

love each other

This is the message you heard from the beginning:
We should love one another.

1 JOHN 3:11 NIV

Too often our blind spots keep us from focusing on others because we're so focused on ourselves. Sure, it's good to do some self-evaluation. But when does that start to shift into self-centeredness? What's the test to see if you are being selfish, jealous, and envious? It's love!

Love has a way of keeping our focus off ourselves. When you truly love someone, your thoughts often start shifting toward them. Romantic love for a partner keeps you going all day, and you can't wait to see them. But a servant love for someone in need gets your gears moving to find creative ways to meet those needs.

Who are you loving today? It's easy to love those who love you back. But what about those who are "unlovable"? Maybe it's someone who has hurt you in the past. It could be someone you just find annoying. Practicing love requires us to love those who may not love us back or are too hard to love in the first place. But that puts you right in position to receive unlimited blessings from God.

keep moving

How can you show love to someone today?

june

friendship

what a great investment

Two are better than one,
because they have a good return for their labor.

ECCLESIASTES 4:9 ISV

Starting a business from scratch can be difficult. First, you need to find the raw materials or the market space. Next, you need to buy goods or equipment to make the products. It can take months before you're even ready to start earning money. But any great idea is worth investing in. That's why a huge part of a business start-up is eyeing investors who can help raise the necessary funds to get going. A great idea is a great investment.

Your dream is a great idea. If it came from God, he has promised success. So what kind of investment are you seeking? The investment of friendship may make the difference. When you go at it all alone, you may get the satisfaction of calling all the shots. But you soon learn you are limited. When you invest in relationships and friendships, you will soon find that you are closer to your goal. And at the same time, you get to help them realize their dream as well. What a great investment!

keep moving

Make a list of close friends with whom you can share your dream.

it's just no good

The Lord God said, "It is not good for the man to be alone. I
will make a helper who is right for him."

GENESIS 2:18 GW

All throughout the creation story, you hear the word *good*.
God looks at the light he created, and he calls it good. He
sees the stars and moon and sun and calls them good. Each
plant that springs up and every animal that crawls on the
ground God calls good. Finally, the crowning achievement
of his work—the creation of humankind. And God calls
that very good.

But then as you keep reading, you find the first
time God calls something no good. He sees some aspect
of his creation that is out of place, and he moves to change
it. What is it? Loneliness. When he sees that Adam has
no partner, God knows that he has to do something. He
decides to create someone who is just right for Adam. He's
done that in your life too. To help you move forward in life,
he will provide you with someone who is just so good for
you. It may be a close friend or relative. It's likely a spouse.
This person will be with you through thick and thin and
will have your back along the way. Thank God he saw what
was no good and turned it into something great!

keep moving
Thank God today for the close friends in your life.

sharper

As iron sharpens iron,
so a friend sharpens a friend.

PROVERBS 27:17 NLT

What good are friends? Sure, they can break up the loneliness of your life. They are trusted companions who have your back. Sometimes it feels like they're just there to take up the space or time you have. But often, those friends act like sharp iron. They rub up against you—either in conflict or comfort—and make you better. They break off the hard edges. They give you wisdom and insight you can't find on your own. Friends just make us better.

When it comes to fulfilling that dream God has placed in your heart, there are lots of reasons to have friends along with you. They will not just help you fight the loneliness or give you a boost during a struggle. There are lessons they can help you learn along the way. There are obstacles that you just can't get over on your own. And your friends will need you as well. You will never fully understand just how much you can sharpen someone else until you try it.

keep moving

Think of one person in your life who can sharpen you while you sharpen them.

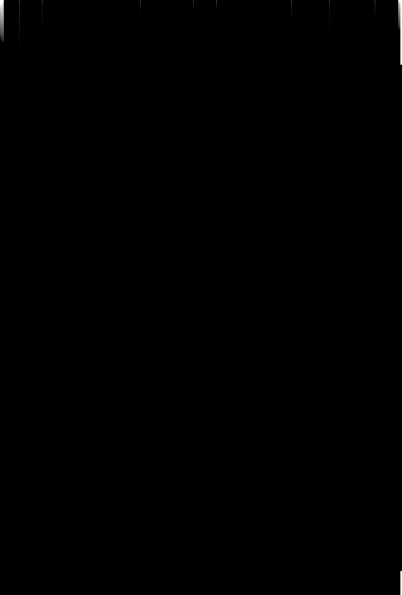

keep your ears open

Listen to advice and accept discipline,
and at the end you will be counted among the wise.

PROVERBS 19:20 NIV

Have you ever been *ghosted*? That's the term people use for when you try to get in touch with someone but they refuse to answer your texts or phone calls. It's like they disappear from your life, just like a ghost. It can be really easy to ghost other people too. Usually it's because they did something that hurt us. But it can also be because they said something that rubbed us the wrong way. Not an insult but a hard truth.

To be wise, we need to keep our ears open to the hard truths in life. If we listen to the advice and discipline of our friends, the hard iron scraping against our edges, then we will be counted among the wise. We will gain so much more insight than if we ghosted them. We will learn things we never knew before. We can start to see the world in a different way. We are more likely to love those who are different from us. And in the end, we will find a true friend who wants to help us become all that God has for us.

keep moving

Think of a time when you received a hard truth but kept your ears open.

a friendly wound

Wounds made by a friend are intended to help,
but an enemy's kisses are too much to bear.

PROVERBS 27:6 GW

Wounds are a sign of hurt, of pain, of mistakes, or of accidents. But they can also be a sign of healing. How can a wound be helpful? One way is from surgery. A doctor may cut into you to correct a problem, leaving behind a wound that heals into a scar. The scar is a reminder of the healing you went through and the problem that was solved.

But can a friend wound you in a helpful way? That's a tough one. Whenever we are hurt by someone we trust, it's almost always bad. It can tear apart a relationship that has taken years to cultivate. But whenever that wounding is for our benefit, it may actually deepen that trust. If a friend tells you a hard truth or confronts you with real conviction, it can feel like a wound at first. Your body does not respond differently to a surgical knife or a carving knife. You feel pain the same way. But in your spirit, you know there is a difference. When you fully understand that a friend who has your best interests in mind has wounded you to help you move forward, you might find that you are actually closer to them than you realize.

keep moving

Has a friend ever wounded you in a way that led to your growth?

a real pick-me-up

*If one person falls, the other can reach out and help.
But someone who falls alone is in real trouble.*

Ecclesiastes 4:10 NLT

They started in the 1980s, the TV commercials that would go viral for several years. "Help! I've fallen, and I can't get up," cried the actress playing the part of an elderly woman living by herself, unable to get back up after a fall. She was all alone, but the medical device she wore around her neck allowed her to call for help. The phrase has gone on to be parodied but proved a remarkable advertising slogan.

There is some spiritual truth behind that commercial. When we are all alone, even the smallest trip can feel like falling into a canyon. Without a friend to pick us back up, we may be stuck. But when we have someone close to us, they can reach down and pick us up. In the same way, we're there for them whenever they need a hand. This type of friendship is never one-sided. There are times when you can help someone else after they receive devastating news. You can share a comforting word. You can reach out with a phone call. You can come by with a meal. And then they return the favor whenever you feel down. That type of friendship is sure to keep you moving forward in life.

keep moving

Name one person whom you could count on if you fall.

consider this

Let us consider how to spur one another on
to love and good deeds.

HEBREWS 10:24 BSB

Have you ever seen an old-time Western movie? They're great
entertainment, mostly because they're pretty predictable.
There will usually be one pivotal scene where the bad guy—
wearing a black hat—is on the run, and the good guy—in a
white hat—has to chase him down. So our hero will jump
on his horse, loosen the reins, and then jab his spurs into the
horse's side. The horse shoots off in hot pursuit!

That's the image that usually comes to mind when
we read the verse above. A spur is not always a pleasant
experience. It's sharp. It jabs us. But it does produce some
kind of result. Here, the writer of Hebrews is encouraging
all of us to help each other toward a shared goal—love and
good deeds. You've likely been spurred on by a manager at
work to complete a task, by a coach to train harder, or even
by a preacher to live right. When it comes to friendship,
someone close to you should have permission to poke at
you to keep moving forward. This type of spur can be the
motivation you need at just the right time to get unstuck.

keep moving

Think of ways to spur each other on to love and
good deeds.

on my honor

Honor your father and your mother so that you may have a
long life in the land that the LORD your God is giving you.

EXODUS 20:12 CSB

We can express honor in a lot of different ways. You can
honor someone by obeying them if they are in a position
of authority over you. You can also honor someone with
respect. That means you treat them fairly, you take care of
their needs, and you talk about them positively to others.
You may not agree with everything they've ever done or
told you, but you don't talk down to them, and you don't
talk about them behind their back. These are just a few
ways to keep that relationship healthy.

But who is "your father and your mother"? Is it only
the biological pair that gave you life? Or should we expand
that meaning? If you come from a nontraditional home, a
parent may be a stepfather or stepmother, perhaps even a
grandparent. And outside of your biological family, you may
have a spiritual parent who has guided you. The promise
of a long, healthy life is true when you honor anyone who
has poured into your life. And that promise extends into
fulfilling the dream God has placed in your heart.

keep moving

Who is someone, other than your biological parent,
who has given you fatherly or motherly love?

encouragement needed

Encourage one another and build each other up,
just as in fact you are doing.

1 THESSALONIANS 5:11 NIV

What does it take to be a good friend? The kind that
sticks close by no matter what. The one who is always
there. Someone whom you want to be around. One of
the essential ingredients is encouragement. To encourage
means to build up whenever we see someone torn down.
If you've ever had a friend who said the right thing at the
right time, then you already know what encouragement is.

Encourage is an interesting word. If you break it
down, it literally means to put courage in someone. When
you are encouraged, you are filled with boldness to dream
big dreams. You are brave enough to face the unknown.
You can endure any struggle. You have tenacity in any
adventure. That's what a close friend gives you. And that's
what you can give a close friend. As you both encourage
each other, you are empowered to reach your goals.

keep moving

How can you encourage someone today?

a heart full of joy

Perfume and incense bring joy to the heart, and the
pleasantness of a friend springs from their heartfelt advice.

PROVERBS 27:9 NIV

Some people love certain smells. Cinnamon can remind
you of a good childhood memory, like baking cookies with
your grandmother. Maybe it's the smell of roses that brings
you back to a fantastic date or the smell of auto grease that
reminds you of your first car. That's the power of smells.
They can instantly transport you into a fond memory and
transform an otherwise dreary day.

Good friends are even better. When you hang out
with old friends, how often do you bring up an old phrase,
an inside joke, or a fond memory? It's often, isn't it? The
pleasantness of a good relationship is not just about feeling
good though. Just being around people you like, and who
like you, can fill your tank. It can encourage you in a tough
moment. It will give you the fuel you need to keep going.
It's no wonder that God tells us not to go it alone. When
we have the pleasant experience of close friends, every
unpleasant experience seems to melt away. And we are left
with assurance and confidence of our next step.

keep moving

Reflect on the last time you spent a pleasant day
with a close friend.

grin and bear it

Bear with one another and forgive any complaint you may have against someone else. Forgive as the Lord forgave you.

COLOSSIANS 3:13 BSB

"Grin and bear it." We often say this to someone going through a tough time who wants to quit. Don't give up; just get through it. But there is another way to look at that phrase. To bear with someone can mean to put up with them, to overlook their faults as you remain close. In this passage, it means to forgive someone. The reason we can is because God first forgave us.

To bear with someone can also mean to barely get along with them. To give them the absolute minimum respect and consideration. To scrape by in life as friends. But when you grin through the situation, you will see that it's more than just getting by. There is an absolute joy in forgiving someone else. It's the basis for all friendships since no one is perfect and all friends will one day do something that hurts you. Instead of holding that grudge, give them a grin and let it go. That way you won't be stuck in an unforgiving attitude.

keep moving

Think of a time when your friend forgave you for something you did.

carry on

Carry one another's burdens;
in this way you will fulfill the law of Christ.

GALATIANS 6:2 CSB

When Jesus was getting ready to leave his disciples on earth, he gave them one final commandment: love one another. That is the law of Christ we read about in the New Testament. It is also Jesus' blueprint for successful friendships.

All of us have issues we are taking care of, struggles we are wrestling with, and faults that we want others to overlook. All together, these form the burdens that we have to lug through life. What if someone helped you shoulder that burden? Someone whom you could call when you mess up. Someone who is there when you have a falling out with another friend. They pick you up and carry you just a little further, past the pain and onto the next phase. Without them supporting us, we may get stuck in a holding pattern. But when we commit to carrying another person's burdens, it creates a safe place for us to release our burdens as well. When you carry one another's burdens, each of you can keep moving down the field.

keep moving

Be on the lookout for someone with a burden you can carry today.

the key to friendship

Love prospers when a fault is forgiven,
but dwelling on it separates close friends.

PROVERBS 17:9 NLT

Have you ever been locked out of your car? It's not only an inconvenience, but it's a bit embarrassing too. You never intended to do it, but now you're standing on the other side of the glass, just inches away from the keys. How did you get into this mess in the first place? In life, we can lock ourselves out of relationships with one bad attitude. When we refuse to forgive, we end up cutting off contact with others. We're the ones on the outside looking in.

The key to unlocking friendship is to forgive and forgive quickly. You don't have to get pulled back into a harmful relationship. But when you overlook little offenses in love, you will be able to continue down the path toward the dream God has for you. No one wants to be stuck, and often we wonder how we got here. It may be that you are overlooking something. There may be some unforgiveness in your life keeping you in neutral. And neutral goes nowhere.

keep moving

Is there something a friend has done that you need to forgive? Forgive them.

keep it together

Make every effort to keep the unity of the Spirit
through the bond of peace.

EPHESIANS 4:3 NIV

Keeping a relationship together requires a few things. It takes time and effort on both of your parts. It takes open lines of communication and shared interests. It takes a forgiving spirit. But most of all, it takes unity.

When you lack unity, your friendships will become unbalanced. If all you do or talk about is what the other person is interested in, then there really isn't unity. But when you share with each other your goals and passions and desires, then you can both move forward in life.

What is your part to play in keeping the unity? It's definitely a two-person operation. Unity is the result of a partnership. It can't be accomplished all alone. But you do play your own role in keeping the peace. When you do that part, then the Holy Spirit will intervene and bind your hearts together for your shared goals. It's up to you to identify and address those issues that are preventing you from keeping the unity.

keep moving

Think about a time when you were at odds with a friend. What role did you play in the disunity?

how good it is

See how good and pleasant it is
when brothers and sisters live together in harmony!

Psalm 133:1 gw

Conflict is such an ugly look. You probably know two people who are not good with each other. They are fighting and talking behind each other's backs. It's not a good look for either of them. But when they reconcile and move forward, it's so good to see. They are finally pleasant to be around.

To come back into unity means you can once again live together in harmony. In music, harmony is not the act of playing the exact same note. You do not have to copy someone else to be in harmony with them. There are notes that clash with each other when played together. But when two people are playing their own tunes in a way that harmonizes, it's such a good sound. When you and a friend harmonize, you don't have to look alike, sound alike, or think alike. But you do have to match each other's beat. There is a way that you can live in harmony with someone else, helping each other with your own individual goals. That is not only good and pleasant but empowering as well.

keep moving

Think of a friend who isn't exactly like you but harmonizes with you.

how we treat each other

Love one another deeply as brothers and sisters.
Take the lead in honoring one another.

ROMANS 12:10 CSB

Think of someone you know who is a good friend. Have you ever sat down and thought about what characteristics set them apart? Are they fun to be around? Maybe they never have a judgmental spirit. Or it could just be that they have a lot in common with you and others. One of the things that is likely true of everyone you consider to be a good friend is that they treat others with respect and honor. They don't laugh behind their backs. They don't spread rumors. And they authentically love others.

The way you treat others can affect your movement in life. Someone with a bad attitude will constantly be spinning their wheels, stuck in a self-centered frame of mind. But genuine love gets you out of the rut because it forces you to focus on others, not yourself. When you can accomplish that, you will be closer to a more mature spirit.

keep moving

What is one way you can honor someone today?

all together

Be happy with those who are happy,
and weep with those who weep.

ROMANS 12:15 NLT

The life of the party! That's what we all want to be, right?
We love getting invited, even if we don't end up going. We
like to be considered someone whom others want to be
around. One way to accomplish this is to get out of your
own headspace and become concerned about others' lives.

When you know someone who is happy, be happy
for them. Rejoice in their good news. Don't point to the
negatives but focus on the positives. Even if you aren't
happy in that moment, don't bring them down.

When you know someone who is weeping, weep
with them. Don't be turned off by their situation. Instead,
encourage them while allowing them space to work
through whatever they are mourning. It's fine to cheer them
up, but don't rush the process either.

These are just two ends of the friendship spectrum.
There are plenty of times when a friend will express an
emotion that you don't automatically share. Instead of
trying to change the way they feel, help them along by
affirming their feelings and sticking with them to the end.

keep moving

The next time someone shares a feeling with you,
hold off on judging them.

run for cover

Above all, keep loving one another earnestly,
since love covers a multitude of sins.

1 PETER 4:8 ESV

What is the sincerest form of love? Is it giving a gift or sharing an encouraging word? Maybe it's doing something nice for someone else. While those are important expressions of love, the truest form of love is forgiveness. Your willingness to overlook someone's mistakes can mean the difference between life and death to your relationship with that person.

We all make mistakes. We all have regrets we would love to keep covered up. A true friend loves despite the faults. And when you love someone enough to forgive them, you will cover up a multitude of sins. That's not to say that their actions have no consequences. If someone intentionally hurts you, there is no standard that says you need to put yourself in danger again. But minor offenses that you overlook can keep the past where it belongs and keep things like jealousy and envy at bay. When you cover up someone else's sins by forgiving them in love, you allow both of you to stay unstuck in life.

keep moving

What is a minor mistake you are glad others covered up for you?

choose wisely

The righteous choose their friends carefully,
but the way of the wicked leads them astray.

PROVERBS 12:26 NIV

Friends are such an important part of our lives. The
company you keep can determine the destiny of your life.
Author and entrepreneur Jim Rohn suggests that we will
become the average of the five people we spend the most
time with. So choose your friends wisely.

First, think about how they treat others. They may
be nice to your face, but if they are talking about others
behind their backs, they may be doing the same to you.
Also consider if the relationship is one-sided. If you feel like
you are the one who is always giving, always sharing, always
there for them, but don't feel there is a return, then you may
be in a lopsided relationship. Another thing to look out for
is any moral failures. Not minor mistakes but obvious sins
that the other person is not addressing.

If you choose your friends wisely, you will find a
companion who can help you move forward in life. Instead
of holding you back, they will propel you into God's great
future for you.

keep moving

What do you look for in a friend?

bad company

Don't fool yourselves.
Bad friends will destroy you.

1 CORINTHIANS 15:33 CEV

Any doctor will agree that diet and exercise are key components to a healthy lifestyle. Eating the right things and staying active will go a long way toward ensuring you a long life. But there are also some things you need to avoid. Cigarettes, excessive drinking, processed foods, poor sleep habits, sitting too much, negative thoughts—all these can steal that good life from you.

The most important reason for choosing good friends is the effect bad friends can have on you. It's not just about surrounding yourself with good friends. It's also about removing bad influences from your life. How can bad company destroy you? They can corrupt your morals. They can seep into your life and change the way you think about God, about others, and about yourself. They can become excuses for living a not-so-great lifestyle. Steer clear if you want to live a life passionately pursuing God's dream for you.

keep moving

How has a bad friendship hurt you in the past?

take your temperature

Don't befriend angry people
or associate with hot-tempered people.

PROVERBS 22:24 NLT

You are what you eat. You're also the average of your five closest friends. Spending time with people allows them to rub off on you. If your friends are caring and loving, you soon will find that you're acting with consideration to others. If your friends are hot-tempered though, you might start flying off the handle at even the smallest issue.

Angry people tend to want company. They like to tell other people how bad their situation is, how hurt they are, and how horribly they've been treated. And they want you to agree. When you get angry, you feel like sharing it, right? But if you find yourself constantly in the company of angry people, it may be time to make some changes. There are difficult conversations ahead and difficult choices to make. But these choices are the most important for you if you want to stay unstuck in life.

keep moving

How can an angry person make you angry too?

where anger lives

Do not be quickly provoked in your spirit,
for anger resides in the lap of fools.

ECCLESIASTES 7:9 NIV

Anger can change you. Anger changes your outlook.
How you view what someone else has done to you will be
amplified if you only see red. Anger changes your thought
life. Instead of focusing on the positive, you find yourself
always pondering the worst-case scenario. Anger changes
your direction in life too. You put yourself at risk of losing
friends and missing out on a bright future if you are always
or easily angered.

The words of wisdom from the Bible tell us that
anger lives in the lap of fools. Frequent outbursts of anger
often define these kinds of people. A person exhibiting road
rage never looks good. A red-faced neighbor is not very
inviting. Are you defined by your anger?

A lot of times we justify our anger. We feel right in
acting angry toward someone. *They cut me off in traffic.*
They shouldn't have said that. They're wrong; I'm right.
However, anger is rarely justified. And a cool temper is
always welcome.

keep moving

What is one thing you do to keep your anger
temperature low?

keep it out of your mouth

Do not use harmful words, but only helpful words, the kind
that build up and provide what is needed, so that what you
say will do good to those who hear you.

EPHESIANS 4:29 GNT

"What did you just say to me?" Those can be fighting words.
Our words have a way of guiding our destiny. What
we say will many times determine what we do. Or just as
serious, what others think about us. If we are gossiping,
lying, or bragging, people won't want to be around us. And
they will likely not want to invest in the dream that God has
placed in our hearts.

When someone makes a remark that we don't like, we
have a choice. Are we going to fire back with an insult, or will
we let cooler heads prevail? We can keep our mouth closed
and suffer the pain of humiliation. But we will also keep our
feet on the right path. Getting into arguments will only take
us off track and offline from God's will for our lives.

keep moving

Think of a time when you replied to someone in
a way you weren't proud of. How could you have
stopped yourself?

the ministry of reconciliation

Everything is from God, who has reconciled us to himself
through Christ and has given us the ministry
of reconciliation.

2 CORINTHIANS 5:18 CSB

Let's say you have two friends. You're good with this friend
and that friend, but they aren't good with each other. It's not
just that they aren't close friends. They're always fighting.
What do you do?

God has called us into a ministry of reconciliation.
It started when he made peace with us through his Son.
When Jesus died on the cross, he brought peace between
you and your heavenly Father. What was separating you
from God, Jesus permanently took care of. No longer did he
hold it against you.

Now that you have peace with God, Jesus wants you
to have peace with others. Maybe you have that, but you
know someone else who doesn't. Perhaps you're in their
lives to make that happen! You can take steps to reconcile
them with each other. Get them together and hash it out.
Or just help them each individually to see where they were
wrong and how they can make it right. Being a minister of
reconciliation is a great way to practice your peacemaking.
And it will surely keep you headed in the right direction.

keep moving

Pray about a friend who may need to reconcile with
another friend.

humble and gentle

Be humble and gentle in every way.
Be patient with each other and lovingly accept each other.
Ephesians 4:2 gw

There are a multitude of characteristics of a good friend.
You don't have to look further than the fruit of the Spirit
in Galatians 5:22–23 to see a great list. Two things that
always seem to come to the surface, though, are humility
and gentleness. Being humble means that you don't always
think of yourself but you consider others. You put them
first. Gentleness is the attitude we should have when
dealing with others, especially when they have wronged us.
Having a humble and gentle spirit is obviously attractive,
and it helps keep you from getting stuck in life.

Acceptance is often a buzzword for being permissive
about another person's sin. You can cover over a multitude
of sins with forgiveness without accepting their sins. But
there is another way to look at the word *acceptance*. Most of
us have flaws that we feel get in the way of being accepted
by others. When we respond to the other person's faults
with humility and gentleness, we are showing them that
we accept them no matter what. Just think of how that will
make them feel, energizing them to keep going in life.

keep moving

What is one way you can be humble and one way
you can be gentle today?

lay it all down

"Greater love has no one than this:
to lay down one's life for one's friends."

JOHN 15:13 NIV

What's the greatest love you've ever received? Was it the love of a parent or grandparent who taught you all you know today? Was it the love of a spouse, fiancé, or fiancée who said, "I do"? Was it the love of a close friend who showed up in the nick of time? All these are great displays of love, but they're not the greatest. There is one thing that one friend did for you that outshines all others. Jesus laid down his life for you, and he did it not out of obligation but for love.

We are taught to live our lives the way Jesus lived his, from our faithfulness to the Father to our gratitude for life. There are so many ways to show the world that we are his followers. But the best way is to lay down our lives. That doesn't mean we have to literally die. But it does require us to die to selfish attitudes, to die to meaningless ambition, to die to worthless arrogance. When we do that, we are truly laying down our lives so that others can live theirs. As we help them move forward in life, we can also chart a path toward God's will for us.

keep moving

What is one way you can lay your life down today?

a friend of God

Scripture was fulfilled that says, "Abraham believed God,
and it was counted to him as righteousness"—
and he was called a friend of God.

JAMES 2:23 ESV

Who's your best friend? What do they mean to you? Where did you meet, and how did you become friends? Of course, this is your best earthly friend we're talking about. We all have the same best friend when it comes to faith. For believers, we are friends of God. And he is our friend as well. We can count him as our best friend. He is always there. He doesn't condemn us for what we've done. He is always loving and always caring. He is sure to help you up when you get knocked down.

Think for a moment what it means to call God "friend." He is the Creator of the universe. He is ruler over heaven and earth. He is the Great I Am, the beginning and the end. But he is also your friend. He is not so big that he can't get down on your level. He is your best friend.

keep moving

Make a list of all the feelings you have about knowing that God is your friend.

face-to-face

The LORD would speak with Moses face-to-face,
just as someone speaks with a friend.

EXODUS 33:11 GNT

The Lord had a very special relationship with Moses. In the Bible, Moses would travel up the mountain to sit in God's presence and talk with him. God would teach him, and Moses would share God's words with the rest of the camp. They had a very personal relationship.

Now, here's the good news. Through Jesus, we have that same relationship. We no longer have to wait for our own Moses to go up a mountain and talk with God. We can speak to him whenever and however we want. He is a friend who will talk to us face-to-face.

Imagine the last time you met up with a friend. As you were talking, you were probably facing each other. If you were sitting side by side, like in a car, you were at least very close. That's how God wants to meet you. He wants to get close to you, be in your space, share life with you. When you accept that invitation, you go from stuck to awestruck!

keep moving

What is one time you felt the personal presence of God?

who's that knocking?

"Look! I stand at the door and knock.
If you hear my voice and open the door, I will come in,
and we will share a meal together as friends."

REVELATION 3:20 NLT

Let's set the scene. You're home all alone. Maybe you just got off work, or perhaps you're in for the night. Picture yourself in your favorite chair when, all of a sudden, there's a knock at the door. Who could it be? It's a surprise, and maybe you're even a little annoyed. You get up to look and find out it's your best friend. Suddenly, you've got a big smile on your face. You open the door and practically drag them in because you're so glad to see them.

This scenario plays out every single day all over the world in the spiritual realm. Jesus stands at our door and knocks. We can let him in if we want to. When we do, he enters as a friend. He sits and spends time with us. He shares with us, he comforts us, he encourages us. Before a new day when you know you'll face challenges, or at the end of a long day working toward that dream God has placed in your heart, it's good to know that you'll have a friend ready to knock at your door.

keep moving

Think of a time when you felt Jesus knocking at your spiritual door.

july

spiritual gifts

information please

About the gifts of the Spirit, brothers and sisters,
I do not want you to be uninformed.

1 Corinthians 12:1 NIV

As believers, we agree on almost everything. A few things seem to bring up a lot more questions than answers though. One such topic is spiritual gifts. Maybe it's because some of us think that our way of interpreting and applying these gifts is the only way. But on the other hand, there is a very simple way to understand spiritual gifts and how they work for our good.

The word *spiritual* refers to several different things. A spiritual gift is a gift from the Holy Spirit. He is the one who imparts these specific talents, abilities, and bents to our lives. *Spiritual* can also mean that these gifts operate on a spiritual plane. They are not normally thought of as physical abilities we are born with. Spiritual gifts are also for our spiritual good, helping us grow.

As we study the spiritual gifts the Lord has given all of us, we are reminded over and over again about just how much he loves us and is cheering us on. He has given us tools we can use to carry out the dream he has planted in our hearts. When you are informed about your specific gifts, you will never want to stop moving forward.

keep moving

What is one misconception you've had about spiritual gifts?

we all get one

God in his kindness
gave each of us different gifts.

ROMANS 12:6 GW

The last time you went to a birthday party, how many
people got gifts? I don't mean the goodie bags that many
parents hand out to their child's friends. I mean wrapped-
up, thought-out presents. Only the birthday boy or girl,
right? In God's grace, he has given a gift to each of us.

You have a spiritual gift. At least one, probably more
than one. No follower of Jesus is left out. Isn't that amazing?
If you never thought of yourself as gifted, now you know
that you are! And each of us has a different gift than our
neighbor, our friends, our family. We don't have to share a
single gift among different people. Our gifts complement
each other's too. That means that one person's gift will fill
in any gaps that another person's gift may overlook. As you
begin to discover your own spiritual gifts, you'll see just
how they complement those around you. And together, you
help each other grow and fulfill the dream God has placed
in your heart.

keep moving

Have you ever done a spiritual gift inventory? What
was the result?

don't neglect it

Do not neglect the spiritual gift you received through the prophecy spoken over you when the elders of the church laid their hands on you.

1 TIMOTHY 4:14 NLT

Timothy was known as Paul's spiritual son. Paul mentored Timothy and had a close relationship with him. So whenever Paul gave Timothy this kind of advice, you know that it came from a heart of deep love and devotion. Paul was not disciplining Timothy for something he failed to do. He was not giving Timothy an ultimatum about what he must do. He was giving Timothy advice on how to do what was deep in Timothy's heart.

Paul knew that God planted a dream in Timothy. He knew how that felt because Paul had a dream too. And he knew what it would take to see that dream come true. Paul told Timothy to use his spiritual gifts, not neglect them, to keep moving forward in life. We can apply this same advice to our own lives. If we neglect the spiritual gifts God has given us, we will inevitably get stuck in a rut. But if we turn to them in times of struggle, we will move forward with confidence.

keep moving

Think of one way you can employ your spiritual gift today.

good gifts

Every good and perfect gift is from above,
coming down from the Father of lights,
who does not change like shifting shadows.

JAMES 1:17 CSB

God knows how to give a good gift. He can outgive anyone you've ever met. He loves to share the best with his children. And he will always have your best interests in mind too.

If you've ever received a good gift, it's godly. That's one way to think of it. If it's good, it's from God. If you have a good job, a good roof over your head, good friends, a good day, those all came from God. And he deserves thanks for them.

The spiritual gifts he gives us are good, too, because they come from our heavenly Father. They are good for us because they help us grow. They are good for us because they make us better. They are good for us because of how great they make us feel. But they are also good for us because they motivate us to action. If you ever feel stuck, you just need to remember the good gifts God has given you, and you'll be back on track in no time.

keep moving

Make a list of the good gifts you've gotten from God in the last week.

out of this world

"Peace I leave with you. My peace I give to you.
I do not give to you as the world gives."

JOHN 14:27 HCSB

One gift that God has given all of us is peace. Not just peace of mind but also peace between us and him. Also he authors peace between us and others. Peace has another component too. The Hebrew word for "peace" is a special one that can also be translated as "completeness" or "wholeness." You are not fully you until you have total peace. And that peace comes from God when we are saved. It's the same peace that reassures us when we face struggles and conflict, knowing that we can make it through anything.

The peace God gives is not like the peace of the world. In fact, it's out of this world! It's so fantastic and unbelievable that no one can fully comprehend it or explain it. The same is true, actually, for every gift God gives. His gifts are all out of this world. That means they are not likely to fail or falter. They will stay with us to the end. You never have to worry about losing any spiritual gift; it's here to stay.

keep moving

Think of a moment when you felt supernatural peace come over you.

no take backs

God doesn't take back the gifts he has given
or disown the people he has chosen.

ROMANS 11:29 CEV

Have you ever had to return something you purchased?
The process can be a little difficult. Some places just ask
you to click a button. Others want to know a lot of details
about why the product didn't work, why you don't want it
anymore, why they should refund your money.

The gifts God has given you are nonreturnable.
They cannot be exchanged or cashed in. They are all yours.
And that's not a bad thing because every gift from God is
actually the perfect fit. Once you discover your spiritual
gifts, you will see just how much they make your life
better. You'll never want to be without them. And God has
promised never to take them away.

Now you know. Whenever you feel stressed, you can
rest assured that God's gifts aren't going to vanish. They
won't leave you. They won't disappear. They are there for
good. You can use them to keep marching forward in life
without fear.

keep moving

Why do you think it's important that God's gifts
are irrevocable?

how do you get it?

I would like to learn just one thing from you:
Did you receive the Spirit by the works of the law,
or by believing what you heard?

GALATIANS 3:2 NIV

Think about the last time you got a birthday gift. Why did you get it? What did you do to earn it? Nothing, right? In fact, it was your mother who did all the work. Maybe she deserves a gift on your birthday.

With God, it's the same way. We don't do anything to deserve or earn a spiritual gift. He gives them to us freely. We don't have to work hard to get them. No amount of obedience to the law will make them ours. Nothing we do will impress God enough so that he's forced to give us even more gifts.

How do we get them? Not by our own actions or merits. But by believing God. When you put all your trust in him, he imparts all your gifts to you. It's just a matter of listening to his voice and responding when he calls. That way you are always ready to move out into the bright future he has planned for you.

keep moving

Have you ever thought you had to earn something from God?

just ask

"As bad as you are, you know how to give good things to your children. How much more, then, will your Father in heaven give good things to those who ask him!"

MATTHEW 7:11 GNT

Scavenger hunts can be a lot of fun. You have to complete a number of tasks to get to the end. The first one to finish gets a prize. And the tasks are often difficult or outrageous, like climbing up a hill or getting a stranger to agree to something. It frequently involves a certain amount of boldness and endurance to get to the end. There are hoops you have to jump through, in other words.

But with God, there are no hoops. He has no obstacle course set up for you to finish to earn your gift. He hasn't laid out a scavenger hunt so you can hopefully find his will for your life. Instead, he gives it readily and freely, no strings attached. All we need to do is ask. If you simply ask him in prayer for what you need—a gift, a healing, a miracle—he is willing to answer.

keep moving

What is one thing you would like to ask God for today?

keep it going

I remind you to fan into flames
the spiritual gift God gave you.

2 Timothy 1:6 NLT

Have you ever been on a campout? There's not a lot to do. Once you have your tent pitched, you can lie back and enjoy the great outdoors. The only concern, really, is the campfire. You have to tend it, turning the logs over and over, making sure you have enough firewood on hand, and stoking the flames to keep them going. Sometimes you can fan the fire to make it hotter, brighter, higher.

That's the picture that Paul left Timothy with. Keep the fire going. Remember to focus on your spiritual growth. Give yourself enough fuel from the Word of God. Make sure the fire doesn't get cold. Turn over to him the things in your life that need to be released. Stoke the flame with zeal once in a while. Put some oxygen into your life by breathing in the Holy Spirit. Utilize those gifts in ways that help others too. If you do this, you'll keep the fire going. And if you keep the fire going, you'll keep going too.

keep moving

What is one way you can fan into flames God's gift today?

same Spirit

There are different kinds of spiritual gifts,
but the same Spirit is the source of them all.

1 CORINTHIANS 12:4 NLT

A lot of people have different ideas and opinions about spiritual gifts. Some think that only a few of them are still in operation today, whereas others believe that all of them are available to every believer. Some think that they need to use their spiritual gifts in any and every church setting while others want to take a more conservative approach.

The gifts God gives are all different too. The variety of abilities and talents God has bestowed on us is almost as limitless as the ideas we each have about those abilities.

But there is one constant. The Holy Spirit is the giver of every gift. If you have a gift and your neighbor has a different one, you both got it from the same Spirit. If you have one idea about how to use your gift and your friend has a different one, you both got those ideas from the same Spirit. In fact, that same Spirit wants you to walk in sameness with your friends and fellow believers. That act of unity is what will keep all of us moving forward to God's will for our lives.

keep moving

What is one act of unity you've seen recently?

what are they good for?

A spiritual gift is given to each of us
so we can help each other.

1 Corinthians 12:7 nlt

Why do you need a spiritual gift? Is it so that you can find a place of service in your church? Maybe. Is it to make you look important or to give you good vibes? Not really. Then why do we have spiritual gifts? There's really only one answer: so we can help each other.

God never meant for you to use your spiritual gifts on yourself. These gifts—and there are at least two lists of them in the New Testament—are all about how you help others. God means for you to share your gifts. He wants you to use them to serve one another. There is no gift that is focused solely on yourself. In fact, if you try to use your spiritual gift only for yourself, if you decide to hoard it so no one else can benefit, that gift will start to atrophy. It will become useless to you. Instead, use your gift to help others achieve their goals. And then let others help you by using their gifts. This is why we have different gifts in the first place: to keep all of us from getting stuck in selfishness.

keep moving

What is a way you can use your spiritual gift to help others?

speak out

*If God has given you the ability to prophesy,
speak out with as much faith as God has given you.*

ROMANS 12:6 NLT

Let's look at the different spiritual gifts in the Bible.
Two places that have lists of gifts are Romans 12 and
1 Corinthians 12. The first gift that Paul talked about
in Romans is the gift of prophecy. There are some
misconceptions about this gift. While some may think
of prophecy as predicting the future, very rarely is that
the case. The simplest definition of a prophet is the man
or woman of God who speaks the message of God to the
people of God.

If you have this gift, then you are probably
already outspoken. Maybe you have lots of opinions and
convictions. You could also be gifted with public speaking.
You might find yourself the center of attention though, if
you don't use this gift wisely. On the other hand, if you hold
back when you feel God telling you to speak out, you won't
be stewarding your gift properly.

Speaking out about things you know to be true can
help you advance your dream and give others insight into
their goals as you put actions behind your words. Allow
God to direct you to those who need to hear what you have
to say, part of the dream God has planted in you.

keep moving

When was a time you felt like speaking out?

service please

If your gift is serving,
then devote yourself to serving.

ROMANS 12:7 GW

Another spiritual gift is service. This may seem like a no-brainer. Aren't we all called to serve one another? Of course. But some of us are gifted in this area more than others. If you have this gift, you are probably an extrovert. You love to throw a party and invite everyone you know. You like to show up early for church events and help set up, staying late to clean up after. This is part of who you are, honestly.

That's what makes spiritual gifts so unique. God has designed us for them. He has hardwired each of us for a perfect fit with the gift he has chosen for us. That's one reason we shouldn't be jealous of another person's spiritual gifts. If we had their gift, we may not be able to use it the right way. But when you lean into your gift, like serving, you can devote yourself completely because you trust God to make the perfect match.

keep moving

How can you serve someone today?

teachers teach

You have often heard me teach. Now I want you to tell these same things to followers who can be trusted to tell others.

2 TIMOTHY 2:2 CEV

The gift of teaching is a lot like the job of teaching. But in some ways, it's completely different. A schoolteacher must know how to lead a classroom of different kids, prepare lesson plans and deliver them, grade assignments, and coordinate with parents. Spiritual teachers are simply called to teach others the things they have learned.

Before Jesus left this earth, he told his disciples to go make more disciples. They were to baptize them and include them in the family of God. Then they were to teach them the same things that Jesus had taught them. The apostles did this through the power of the Holy Spirit. Without the spiritual gift of teaching, we are just imparting knowledge. With the Spirit's help, we are unlocking the future. We are casting a vision from one generation to the next, from one group to another. And we are unlocking our own potential as well. We are making a way to get unstuck and move into a great future for ourselves.

keep moving

Do you think you could be a teacher, or does it intimidate you? Why or why not?

encourage

If your gift is to encourage others,
be encouraging.

ROMANS 12:8 NLT

We all need encouragement now and then. None of us are fully self-reliant. We lean on each other in our struggles. We reach out for healing of hurts. We tend to feel better when someone asks us how we're doing. It's common for all of us.

What is often uncommon is the encouragement side. It's hard to know the right thing to say at the right time. It's tough to always be looking for those who need the pick-me-up. But for those who are fully committed to pursuing God's dream for their lives, encouragement can be like jet fuel. It can motivate you to continue in your journey. When you encourage someone else, it does something inside you. It brings you joy to see that you are bringing joy to others. It lights you up when you see someone else light up because of what you said.

For some of us, we're naturally gifted by the Holy Spirit to do this. For the rest of us, encouraging others shouldn't be something we ignore. Being an encourager is something anyone can be.

keep moving

How have you been encouraged lately?

on the giving end

Each of you should give what you have decided in your heart to give, not reluctantly or under compulsion, for God loves a cheerful giver.

2 CORINTHIANS 9:7 NIV

Being generous doesn't take a gift of the Spirit. It just takes determining why and how you give. Any of us can be a blessing to those around us. And all of us have been called to give part of what we've been given.

However, some are supernaturally gifted at this. The gift of being a giver is truly transformational. As you pursue God's plan for your life, consider what you are giving back while God is currently blessing you. Find a way to start making investments in his kingdom now. And as you do, he will return that gift in the form of divine intervention and empowerment. Give to others who are also pursuing their dream, and you'll find your dream closer within reach. God loves it when you give with the right attitude and plenty of heart. So don't delay; start now.

keep moving

How can you start increasing the way you give to God?

on the leader ship

If God has given you leadership ability,
take the responsibility seriously.

Romans 12:8 NLT

We cannot all be leaders. God has given to the church apostles, prophets, evangelists, pastors, and teachers. These are specific offices and officers whom God has called into leadership positions. There are other leaders he has called too. He has called CEOs and managers in the business world to partner with churches to help fulfill God's dream. He has called homemakers and entrepreneurs to leverage their influence for the kingdom.

In what way are you a leader? You may not own a business or have a wide footprint on social media. But there are ways you can seriously lead others. Maybe there is just one person whom you can mentor and show them how you've accomplished what you have so far. One way to look at it is to find someone who is further ahead of you who can mentor you while finding someone else who is further behind you whom you can mentor. As you pull them along, you also will be pulled along.

keep moving

Do you consider yourself a leader? Why or why not?

so kind

Whoever shows kindness to others
should do it cheerfully.

ROMANS 12:8 GNT

Kindness is both a fruit of the Spirit and a gift of the Spirit. This can be a little difficult to grasp. In other words, we are all called and empowered to be kind to one another. But some of us can do it pretty easily. They are given a specific gift of sharing a kind word, acting in a kind way, and showing a kind smile.

The trick is that many times people with the gift of kindness can feel like others take advantage of them. They give and give without getting much in return. They will work for free, from the goodness of their heart. They will gladly share with others even when others don't share. That's why the Bible warns us to show kindness with cheer. There is a temptation to expect something in return when we are kind. Instead, we should see that the reward is the Holy Spirit's power active in our lives to help us move forward.

keep moving

When have you shown kindness to someone who did not seem to be grateful afterward?

it's not just what you know

To one person the Spirit gives the ability to give wise advice;
to another the same Spirit gives a message of special
knowledge.

1 Corinthians 12:8 NLT

Another list of spiritual gifts starts with spiritual wisdom and special knowledge. While it may seem like this gift is all about imparting secret knowledge, it's really about how you use what God has revealed to you. Nothing the Holy Spirit tells us will contradict what we already know from his Word. And everything he tells us will bring glory to Jesus and honor to others.

It's important to realize that wisdom and knowledge are more than just what you can know. It's also how you use it. Applying the Word of God is the point of instruction. Jesus said that the wise person hears what God says and then puts it to use. When we do that, we will find ourselves getting out of any rut we end up in.

If you have this spiritual gift, make sure that you are using it with both humility and accuracy. Put it to good use. Be bold in how you tell others what God has told you. But be careful of any tendency toward pride.

keep moving

When have you felt like you got a special word of
knowledge or wisdom from God?

faith to believe and power to heal

One and the same Spirit gives faith to one person,
while to another person he gives the power to heal.

1 Corinthians 12:9 gnt

God wants to see you whole. He loves it when you get over a pain or past hurt. It may be mental, emotional, spiritual, or physical. And he has decided to give certain people the spiritual gift to bring that about. It may seem strange to hear, but there are believers who are specifically chosen to pray for others to bring healing.

The Bible says that if we are in need of healing, we should call on the elders of the church to pray for us. If you have a need today, seek out the help of others. If you feel stuck, turn to someone who may be gifted with greater faith to help you get moving. It's not embarrassing to admit you need help. All of us are hurting at some point in our lives. And if no one asked for help, then those who are gifted would not be able to use their gifts. They might get stuck along with us.

keep moving

What is something that you need someone else to pray for right now?

it's a miracle!

God did extraordinary miracles through Paul.

ACTS 19:11 NIV

Along with the gift of faith and healing is the gift of miracles. It may seem that this is just the same miraculous healing power. But there is a slight difference. Nearly every time this word is used in the New Testament, it's in reference to casting out a demon or destroying the works of Satan.

There is a real enemy who wants to slow you down and keep you stuck. You have authority in God over any demonic attack. Some, though, have been supernaturally gifted to work miracles in the spiritual realm. Their job is to help those who have been hamstrung by the Enemy. The way he attacks, like a roaring lion, is to get us all alone and take us out one by one. But when we work together, those who have faith, those who have the gift of miracles, those blessed with the gift of kindness can form an army against him. We can fight for each other and keep each other moving forward in this world. Nothing can stop us if we truly believe in the miracle-working power of God.

keep moving

Have you ever had an encounter that you had no explanation for other than the supernatural?

great insight

He gives one person the power to perform miracles, and
another the ability to prophesy. He gives someone else the
ability to discern whether a message is from the Spirit of
God or from another spirit.

1 CORINTHIANS 12:10 NLT

Another spiritual gift on this list is the ability of spiritual
discernment. This one often goes hand in hand with the
gift of prophecy. When we think of prophecy, we also
think of the great insight a prophet has. They have access
to the Word of God, often through the Spirit of God. They
have been given the gift of hearing the Word clearly and
presenting the Word clearly.

In order to be a prophet, you must keep yourself
untainted by the world. If there is any interference from
sin, you may not get the whole message. It could be lost in
translation, or you might be hampered from delivering it.
That's why it's so important not to be dragged down by sin
in your life. For any spiritual gift to be fully activated in your
life, you must be willing to leave your old life behind. You
must have a heart devoted toward the things of God and his
holiness. Otherwise, you will just be spinning your wheels.

keep moving

Is there something you need to ask forgiveness for
that may be keeping you from all God has for you?

let's be clear

Still another person is given the ability to speak in unknown languages, while another is given the ability to interpret what is being said.

1 CORINTHIANS 12:10 NLT

The most controversial spiritual gift has to be the gift of tongues and interpretation. But no discussion about spiritual gifts is complete without addressing it. First, this gift was in use at the time of the apostles. Whether it's still in use today and what form it would take are just two of the questions surrounding this ability.

What most Christians agree on is that if the gift of tongues ever causes confusion in any setting, it should be silenced. In fact, Paul listed speaking in tongues right alongside interpreting, and then he later spent some time explaining these in more detail (1 Corinthians 14). What we know is that clarity of the message matters.

Clearly expressing what God is telling you will often help you move toward the dream God has placed in your heart. Any lack of clarity can keep you stuck where you are. And when you are unable to explain clearly to others where you are going or what you want to accomplish, they won't be able to help you either. Our God is a God of order and clarity, so always seek to understand him completely.

keep moving

What is one thing that you are absolutely clear about when it comes to God?

put them to use

Each of you should use whatever gift you have received to serve others, as faithful stewards of God's grace in its various forms.

1 PETER 4:10 NIV

What good is a tool if it sits in your toolbox and is never used? If you buy a kitchen gadget and it never moves from your junk drawer, is it helpful at all? You may intend to use it someday, but if that day never comes, was it worth investing in?

God has invested in you. He has placed a good gift in your spirit and a great dream in your heart. He is urging you on to the place he wants you to go, and he is giving you the tools to get there. Still, it's up to you to make the moves. If you never use the spiritual gift he's given you, you'll be stuck right where you are.

Being a faithful steward is about more than money. It's about the prudent management of anything we have received from God. That includes the good gifts he has given all of us. In fact, we have an obligation to each other to use our gifts. That's because, primarily, our gifts are meant to serve others. God has designed your gifts for you to use alongside others. And you use them perfectly when they bring glory to God.

keep moving

What is one gift that you may have neglected?

to the best of your abilities

"See...I've filled him with the Spirit of God, giving him skill and know-how and expertise in every kind of craft."

Exodus 31:1–5 MSG

In the Old Testament, before Jesus' death, resurrection, and ascension, the Holy Spirit would come on some people at certain times for specific reasons. You can read about that happening in Exodus when craftsmen were appointed to create the tabernacle and all the instruments of worship. But there were other times when people prophesied or fought in battle under the power of the Holy Spirit.

When Jesus left earth, he asked the Father to send the Holy Spirit. At that moment, his Spirit was poured out on all of us. If you are a believer, you have access to his power twenty-four hours a day, seven days a week. He no longer operates under the old rules. And that means that you may be gifted with certain abilities like a craftsman. Could it be that your knack at computers, your eye for design, your carpentry skill, or your sewing passion is a gift of the Spirit? Maybe. If it brings glory to God and helps others, then definitely. There is an infinite number of ways you can help others fulfill their destiny in God and at the same time keep moving toward your goal.

keep moving

What is one special natural ability you have that you think may be from God?

what's the point?

If anyone speaks, let it be as one who speaks God's words;
if anyone serves, let it be from the strength God provides,
so that God may be glorified through Jesus Christ in
everything. To him be the glory and the power forever and
ever. Amen.

1 PETER 4:11 CSB

There is one main focus of every single spiritual gift. There
is a single purpose for all the different abilities he has given
us. The answer is Jesus. When God is glorified through
Jesus Christ, then we are using our gifts the right way. The
point is never to bring glory to ourselves, to brag on others,
or to make our group feel good. It's all about Jesus.

The thing is, when you use your gifts to glorify God,
you will also share in his glory. If you try to take credit for
everything, then you may receive nothing. You'll be stuck
in your own selfishness. But when you commit to pointing
your gifts outward, showing the world how great God is,
then you will be propelled into your God-given dream.
There is nothing you can't accomplish. Why? Because God
is committed to bringing glory to Jesus so that the whole
world will know him. If you align your personal vision with
the glorification of Jesus, then God will be on your side.

keep moving

What is one way you can use a gift, skill, or ability to
bring glory to Jesus today?

zeal

Never be lacking in zeal,
but keep your spiritual fervor,
serving the Lord.

ROMANS 12:11 NIV

What is zeal? It's an eager desire. It's a fervor for a certain thing. It's a passion that is unrelenting. It's fuel for the fire of your soul. Zeal is the never-ending, always ready, supernatural desire to see God's work come alive through your life.

We can easily start lagging in the zeal department. It's not hard to get off track in life. When we face one too many struggles, we may want to quit. Or at least just take a break. That break could last a long time though. It could mean the difference between finishing well or not finishing at all.

To keep your zeal going, learn how to serve the Lord at all times. While you do need to take breaks now and then, it's not too much to keep yourself on track in life. The zeal of the Lord will fill you as you serve him. And then you will find new energy to keep moving.

keep moving

Think of a time when you lacked zeal. What did you do to get out of that mindset?

poured out

"It will come about at a later time that I will pour out my Spirit on every person. Your sons and your daughters will prophesy. Your elderly people will dream dreams, and your young people will see visions."

JOEL 2:28 ISV

God has poured out his Spirit on every person who believes in him and follows his Son, Jesus. On the day of Pentecost (Acts 2) we find the fulfillment of this very passage of Scripture. And that same promise is for today as well.

Notice that no one is left out. First, God granted the Holy Spirit to sons and daughters. There is no distinction of gender when it comes to spiritual gifts. No particular gift is off-limits to someone because they are a male or female. Second, the old as well as the young have access. There is no expiration date on spiritual gifts. If you feel like you have missed your moment, are past your prime, or have fallen short of fulfillment, God's Word says that's not true. He still has a great plan for your life. Nothing can hold you back if you just believe in him and lean into his dream for your life.

keep moving

What is one thing you thought you wouldn't accomplish because you waited too long?

an act of generosity

He has given each one of us a special gift
through the generosity of Christ.

EPHESIANS 4:7 NLT

"Not too much." That's something a parent might have said
to you as a child while you were pouring out a drink. They
were concerned you would get too much and wouldn't be
able to finish it all. Or maybe they knew that lots of sugary
drinks are bad for you.

But "not too much" is not something that God said
when he poured his Spirit on you. He was not concerned
that you would have too much of your spiritual gift. He
wasn't worried that you would be overflowing in it. In fact,
that's the whole point.

The Bible calls this the generosity of Christ. It's an
extravagant way of giving. It goes beyond normal human
limits and fills us up beyond measure. And it's what God
loves to do. He wants to show you just how much he loves
you by how much he can give you. Enjoy the gracious
special gift of God in abundance.

keep moving

Have you ever been afraid that you wouldn't have
enough from God?

confirmation

God confirmed the message by giving signs and wonders
and various miracles and gifts of the Holy Spirit
whenever he chose.

HEBREWS 2:4 NLT

God's gifts confirm God's message. They go together. He
will pour out his Spirit on everyone who is committed to
following him and sharing his Word with others. When you
do that, he will lavish his gifts on you.

God's message to us is confirmed through spiritual
means. It may not always be visible or overt. It may be a
small voice you hear within. It may even be just for one
person. But God will always be present. If you've ever
shared Jesus with others, you know this to be true. There
are a million stories of someone giving a testimony at just
the right time, saying just the right thing for one particular
person. It can change their whole life. And yours. Knowing
that God will confirm his message will give you boldness
to pursue your passions as they align with your mission to
give glory to Jesus.

keep moving

What is one confirmation you've experienced while
sharing or hearing the Word of God?

the most helpful

You should earnestly desire the most helpful gifts.
But now let me show you a way of life that is best of all.

1 CORINTHIANS 12:31 NLT

"I want that!" It's something a child says in the toy aisle of any department store you visit. It's also what you might say as you scroll through the website of your favorite online retail store. It's often what we say to God too.

It's easy to be jealous of someone else's gift. You see what God is doing through them, and you want that for yourself. But God has already chosen something for you. He has designed you with a particular gift in mind. He wants you to have what is the very best and the most helpful you could possibly enjoy. To want something else would be to want less for yourself.

You will only be stuck if you are jealous of another's gifts. First, you will be focused on what you don't have rather than what you do have. Your attitude will suffer, and you will be left short of what God has in store. Second, you will miss out on how much you can do with the gifts you do have. You might not be able to see just how God will use the gifts he's given you to accomplish your dream. Don't miss out!

keep moving

Think of a time when you were jealous of another person's gifts. Was it helpful or harmful?

august

faith and good works

it's not you

You were saved by faith in God...This is God's gift to you,
and not anything you have done on your own.

EPHESIANS 2:8 CEV

"I've got good news and bad news. Which do you want first?"

It's not often that you only get good news. More often than not, we only hear the bad. But what about those times when the good news and the bad news are the same news? That's never happened to you? Well, it's actually happened to all of us. You see, when God saved you, it was a good news/bad news situation. The bad news is that you played no role whatsoever in your salvation. You couldn't! You were completely powerless. But the good news? It's that you played no role whatsoever in your salvation. God did it all for you.

God saved you through faith as an act of kindness. You had nothing to do with it. Being saved is a gift from God. The fact that the good news and bad news are the same news is actually great news. None of us can save ourselves, and God knew this. Rather than leave us stuck in our sins, though, he made a way. When you rely on him for salvation—our part—he cleanses us from sin and gives us a bright, new future—his part.

keep moving

Take a moment to reflect on the idea that you did nothing at all to earn salvation.

real faith

Faith is confidence in what we hope for and assurance about what we do not see.

HEBREWS 11:1 NIV

We talk a lot about faith. You can use it like a noun, as in the faith you have in God. Or you can even use faith as a synonym for *religion*, as in the Christian faith. You can do it, such as when you say you are putting your faith in someone or something. You might even use it like an adjective, like when you call someone a faithful friend.

But what is faith really? It's complete trust that someone or something will do what you expect them to do. In other words, it's not proof that it will happen. It's the next best thing. Faith means that you can base your entire life around the certainty of that thing happening. We have faith that the sun will rise tomorrow. You put faith in your car starting every morning. Neither of those is guaranteed, and in a way, they are unseen.

The Bible says that faith is venturing out into the unknown with confidence (see Hebrews 11:1). It's about knowing what you cannot see and cannot prove. It's the precursor to hope. Without faith, we are lost because we don't know how to move forward. With faith, we can make confident steps in the right direction.

keep moving

What is one thing about God that you have faith in?

live by faith

"Behold, his soul is puffed up;
it is not upright within him,
but the righteous shall live by his faith."

HABAKKUK 2:4 ESV

Christians should be marked by a lifestyle of faith. Others like to live a lifestyle of luxury. There's also the lifestyle of frugality. And we all remember the lifestyles of the rich and famous. What lifestyle are you living by?

When you trust in your own ability to get yourself out of a jam, to find your own footing, and to make your own decisions, you can easily become puffed up. Arrogance and pride are the earmarks of a lifestyle lived selfishly. And the fall from such a lifestyle is sudden and abrupt.

But when you live by faith, you will keep moving forward in life. Faith involves admitting you don't have it all together, but you don't need to. Faith means you are committed to something greater than yourself. Faith is believing God's best for you. When you live by these principles and others you never have to stay stuck.

keep moving

What is one characteristic of faith that you live by?

walk it out

We walk by faith,
not by sight.

2 CORINTHIANS 5:7 BSB

Cardiologists will tell you that walking is one of the greatest forms of exercise. It gets your heart rate up to a healthy level. It is also low impact, saving your joints and allowing you to go for longer periods of time. With just half an hour a day, walking can add years to your life.

Walking is not just an exercise. Walking is also one way we get around. And it's the analogy used in Scripture for how we live. We each have our own unique gait. And we also have a personal way to live out our lives. One thing that everyone's walk should have is faith.

When we walk by faith, we no longer depend on our sight. That doesn't mean we don't pay attention. It means that we don't see the smallest hurdle ahead as an insurmountable obstacle. We can find ways around, over, or through our problems. We start to live out our God-given dream as we walk out our God-ordained faith. And that can make the difference in how far we end up going in life.

keep moving

What is one way to "walk out" your faith today?

moving mountains

> "Have faith in God. I tell you the truth, you can say to this mountain, 'May you be lifted up and thrown into the sea,' and it will happen. But you must really believe it will happen and have no doubt in your heart."
>
> MARK 11:22-23 NLT

What's the most you've ever lifted? A hundred pounds? A couch? All the groceries into the house in one try? You may be a bodybuilder or just an average person, but there is some limit to your ability to pick things up. No one has ever been able to move a whole mountain. At least not physically. But every day, people of faith move mountains.

Whenever you get stuck, look to see if there is something in your way. Maybe it's anxiety about an upcoming doctor's visit. It could be a problem you've had with someone else. There may be a spiritual issue at play as well. Whatever it is, it can and will move when you apply the power of faith to it.

Doubt is the kryptonite to faith. It's not just a sudden thought that maybe it won't happen. It's a prolonged attitude that God won't do it. It's thinking that God has no interest in helping us move our mountains in life. But he does because he loves you and wants to see every obstacle taken out of your path.

keep moving

What is a mountain in your life that you need God to move?

it's impossible

> It is impossible to please God without faith. Anyone who
> wants to come to him must believe that God exists and that
> he rewards those who sincerely seek him.
>
> HEBREWS 11:6 NLT

Impossible is a big word. The words *likely* and *kinda* have
nothing on *impossible*. It's a stone-cold lock. It's a certainty.
It's written in permanent marker. The Bible says that it is
impossible to please God if you don't have faith.

Now, the first thing that comes to mind is that we
can't make God happy. That's what *to please* means after all.
If you want to please a friend, you might buy them a gift.
But the word for "please" is about the relationship between a
servant and a master. A master is pleased with their servants
when the servants do what they are assigned to do. When
you walk in faith toward the goal God has placed in front of
you, you will please him as a good and faithful servant.

So how does faith actually please God? It's the fuel to
our future. Faith gives us the direction and motivation in life
to keep on moving. Rather than being stuck in place, we move
freely into a bright future. You can't do that without faith.

keep moving

What is one way you can please God today?

justified

We see that people are acceptable to God because they
have faith, and not because they obey the Law.

ROMANS 3:28 CEV

Some words in the Bible need no explanation. They are
simple to grasp. They make perfect sense to anyone when
they first hear them. But there are other words that need a
bit more context. One of those words is *justified*.

When you first hear the word *justified*, you might
think of justifying your own actions. If you can come up
with a good reason for why you did something, you will get
out of trouble. You can justify your own bad attitude, your
own bad behavior. But that's not what the biblical word for
"justified" means.

Different translations of the Bible will interpret this
word in different ways to help us understand. In the verse
above, the word has been translated as "acceptable." On our
own, we are not acceptable to God. Our sin nature just gets
in the way. But once we come to him in faith, he receives us
fully forgiven. We are now acceptable, not because we got
ourselves cleaned up but because we put ourselves in his
hands. And that's the best place to be.

keep moving

What is one way you are justified by God?

all things

Jesus looked at them and said, "With man it is impossible, but not with God. For all things are possible with God."

MARK 10:27 ESV

What would you do if money were no object? Where would you travel to? What would you buy? Another way to put it is to ask what kind of job you would have. If you didn't have to worry about making enough money to live, what type of dream job would you want?

We often ask these types of questions like little mental exercises. There's never a right or wrong answer. You can get to know someone, what they like and who they care about, by asking them a question like this. But more to the point, you can tell where they are going.

You see, with God, nothing is impossible. The avenue in front of us is endless. There are so many options ahead. And they are lined up by God. He's just waiting for us to ask in faith. If you believe that he has your best at heart, then you can ask for the impossible, and he will deliver it.

keep moving

What is one thing you can ask God for that seems impossible?

what have you heard?

Faith comes from hearing, that is,
hearing the Good News about Christ.

ROMANS 10:17 NLT

If you want to grow muscle mass, you work out. If you want your savings account to grow, you have to budget. If you want to grow in IQ, you need to study. But what about faith? Does it grow? Of course it does. But how?

The Bible is foundational to how we grow as believers. Not just because it tells us what we need for salvation but also because it instructs us how to follow him after we've made a declaration of faith. The more time you spend in the Word, the more your faith will grow.

First, you will hear story after story of faith people—those who believed in God and saw incredible things. If they did it, so can you. Another way your faith grows is by reading the great words of praise about God in the Bible. There is something transformative about hearing others give glory to God. Finally, your faith grows when you put what you hear from God into action. If you feel stuck, go back to the last thing you heard from God. Get moving in faith to get out of that rut.

keep moving

When do you like to read the Bible?

what faith does

We remember before our God and Father your work produced by faith, your labor prompted by love, and your endurance inspired by hope in our Lord Jesus Christ.

1 Thessalonians 1:3 NIV

Faith, hope, and love. You'll see these three grouped together in a few places throughout the Bible. You could say they like to hang out. There's a lot connecting all three. You can have faith that God has forgiven your past. You can hope for a bright tomorrow. And you can understand his love.

Faith does something too. It's not just an object or a way of thinking. It's active. Faith produces works. It causes us to serve others. It motivates us to move. And that same faith spurs on labor through love. Your work is not in vain if you are motivated by faith and love. Finally, you can endure any trial thanks to faithful hope. When you put all your trust in God for your future, he will stand by it.

Work produced by faith, labor prompted by love, and endurance inspired by hope. Those are three things you can use every day.

keep moving

Which of these three values best resonates with you?

when he believed

Abram believed the LORD, and the LORD counted him
as righteous because of his faith.

GENESIS 15:6 NLT

There are moments in your life that will define you. You
can mark these on your life's calendar with a long, red
line. Everything before it is the way you were. Everything
after it is the way you are. Nothing is the same. It's all been
changed. That's what happened to Abraham.

God spoke to Abraham (here called Abram) to
leave his land, his family, whatever was familiar, and go to
another place that God would show him. When Abraham
arrived at this place, God promised to make him a great
father, the leader of an entire nation. Abraham had every
reason to doubt. He was all alone, and his wife was barren.
Huge hurdles! But he believed anyway.

What happened when he believed? God called him
righteous. That word means a lot of different things. It can
mean that he was morally upstanding. It can also mean he
was accepted by God. Both are true here. Because Abraham
believed in God, God was pleased with him. Because
Abraham pleased God, God empowered him. Because
Abraham was empowered by God, he was able to make right
decisions. And the line that Abraham drew was a line of faith.

keep moving

Can you point to the faith line that was drawn in
your life?

faith to faith

In the gospel God's righteousness is being revealed from faith to faith, as it is written, "The righteous will live by faith."

ROMANS 1:17 ISV

Is there an end point to faith? I don't mean is their faith after your time on earth is over. I mean if you have faith in God for something, is there a point where that faith runs out? This verse seems to say that's not the case. In fact, you go "from faith to faith." From faith for one thing to faith for another. It's ever increasing and always expanding. The faith you have for today will lead to faith in a hope for tomorrow.

The faith you have now may be small. It could be just a glimmer of the big picture God has for you. He planted a dream in your heart, but you're not sure you will be able to see the whole thing come to pass. Take a moment to find one part of that dream you can accomplish. Believe God for that one thing. And then let that faith move to another faith. Faith in the next step. And the next step after. And soon you will find yourself running with faith toward the goal.

keep moving

What is one small thing for which you can have faith in God today?

he enables you

The Sovereign Lord is my strength;
he makes my feet like the feet of a deer,
he enables me to tread on the heights.

HABAKKUK 3:19 NIV

Maybe you're a runner. Maybe you're not. If you are, then you know the importance of a good pair of shoes. Not only do they keep you from hurting your feet, but they can also help you control your pace. A good shoe has tread that grips the ground to help you move forward more quickly and more assuredly. That's what faith does for our spiritual lives.

The Lord is the one who enables you. He will give you strength when you feel like you're slipping. He will sustain you through the darkest night. He will comfort you when you feel like giving up. He will give you grip when the road gets steep.

Notice that the prophet said that it is the sovereign Lord who does this. *Sovereign* means "in control." We don't push a button or provide any guidance. He is the one who is behind the scenes making this happen. It's his desire and his delight to. There is nothing you need to do except ask him. He is ready to give you rest from your journey and strength for the next.

keep moving

How have you seen the sovereign Lord working in your life?

cover up

In the cool of the evening, the man and his wife heard the
Lord God walking around in the garden. So they hid from
the Lord God among the trees in the garden.

GENESIS 3:8 GW

Adam and Eve had messed up. They disobeyed God. They
did the one thing he told them not to. And because of that,
they felt shame. They looked at themselves and saw that
they were naked, so they tried to cover up and hide. But the
covering they made for themselves was insufficient. They
used fig leaves to cover up. Little was left to the imagination
though. They were still naked before God.

There is no hiding from God. Not really. We can try
to obscure who we are, but he sees our heart. As Adam and
Eve came out from their hiding place, God first disciplined
them for their sin. What he did next illustrates exactly
the portrait of what could happen for us internally if we
choose. God created for them clothing out of animal hide.
The clothing they had made for themselves didn't work. It
wasn't strong enough to withstand storms and struggles.
But what God provided was more than adequate.

Are we still trying to hide today? We all have places
in our lives that are insufficient, falling short. But God's
adequacy covers even the worst of our past.

keep moving

How do you try to hide your inadequacy from God
and others?

failure is not final

The godly may trip seven times, but they will get up again.
But one disaster is enough to overthrow the wicked.

PROVERBS 24:16 NLT

Every success story is a string of failures leading to an ultimate victory. What every successful individual has in common with each other is not unlimited resources, unsurpassed talent, or unrelenting ideas. It's that they all got up again when they failed. If you're trying to avoid mistakes thinking that one slipup will set you too far back, you're missing the point. We all make mistakes.

We like to view our heroes in the best light possible. But it's when we are honest about their failures that we have confidence to see our own failures through God's sight. He loves and cares for you. He takes no joy in watching you mess up. He can turn each failure into a lesson that moves you closer to success. Every hero has a moment or moments when they want to give up. The going has always been tough, but at that time it seems impossible. It's in those moments that the hero will rise one more time and see his or her dream come true. Are you at that moment yet? Are you ready to keep going?

keep moving

What failure in your past led to success later?

stop hiding

He answered, "I heard you in the garden,
and I was afraid because I was naked; so I hid."

GENESIS 3:10 NIV

The story of Adam and Eve is interesting. They had a face-to-face relationship with God. They walked with him and talked with him. He had one rule, but they broke it and were scared—so they hid. That is an attribute that found its way deep down into the human DNA. Often when we sin, we find a way to justify it or hide it from God.

You will experience incredible breakthrough in your life if you decide to come out from hiding and into a place of radical honesty with God and yourself. That place of honesty will allow you to wrestle with real truth, and real truth will set you free.

To understand how to get to radical honesty, we first have to realize we have a natural propensity to hide from the truth. It's in our genes. But God's very nature is to forgive. We must stop hiding who we are from the one who sees us as we are. And he is also the one who loves us as we are. If we ever hope to change, we must first admit that we need change.

keep moving

What part of you do you try to hide from the world?

fatal mistakes

The LORD's anger burned against Uzzah,
and God struck him dead on the spot for his irreverence,
and he died there next to the ark of God.

2 SAMUEL 6:7 CSB

David's life story in the Bible is riddled with failure. He
committed adultery with Bathsheba. That was tragic
enough. But his failures also put others in danger. In 2
Samuel 6, a story plays out that started with good intentions
but ended in disastrous consequences.

At that time, the ark of the Lord, which symbolized
the presence of God, had been missing in action. Taken
by the Philistines, it eventually ended up in the hands of
some townsfolk. When David heard this, he wanted to do
what was right and bring it back to the tabernacle. Only
the priests were supposed to carry the ark, but David put
it on a cart instead. It hit a bump, and a man named Uzzah
tried to steady it. This killed him because he was not a
priest. David should have transported the ark the way God
had commanded. David went into a time of repenting and
confessing his sin for not caring for God's presence like he
should have. God was gracious to forgive. If you haven't
handled the gifts, blessings, and time that God has given
you, there is still time for you to correct your course.

keep moving

What mistake have you made in the past that you
thought was final?

admit your mistakes

If we admit our sins—simply come clean about them—
he won't let us down; he'll be true to himself.
He'll forgive our sins and purge us of all wrongdoing.

1 JOHN 1:8-10 MSG

The first step in turning failure into success is to look at ourselves and find any fault within. This is best done with the aid of divine insight. Asking the Holy Spirit to search our hearts is not about him seeing if we have done wrong, but it's about him showing us where we've done wrong.

David had a hard time doing this. What was his first response when God struck down Uzzah for touching the ark? Anger. David was enraged. At himself? Nope. He was mad at God. He was so mad that he abandoned his plan to return the ark to Jerusalem. In other words, his anger, brought on by a refusal to admit he was wrong, kept him stuck.

We often want to find blame in someone else. We love to deflect our own mistakes outward. There is a real fear involved in this. If we admit that we messed up, then maybe we're admitting that we are a mess-up. But freedom is found on the other side of responsibility. If we admit our shortcomings, God is faithful to make up the rest through his forgiveness.

keep moving

Ask the Holy Spirit to search you for any hidden sin
or fault, then come clean about it.

quit replaying your past

Forgetting the past and looking forward to what lies ahead,
I press on to reach the end of the race and receive the
heavenly prize for which God, through Christ Jesus,
is calling us.

PHILIPPIANS 3:13–14 NLT

Regrets can be hard to get over. Researchers have found that
we are better at remembering the bad things we do than the
good things that happen to us. And it's compounded over
and over again. There's a little voice in your head telling
you that you're not good enough, that you'll always come
up short. That voice uses your memories against you. It
dredges up past mistakes and drags you down when you
think about your future. That voice is not lying to you, but
it's only telling you half the truth.

People may love to remind you of when you failed.
They may stay quiet about your success though. Don't let
that affect you. Your failure does not define you. Your future
is not determined by a past mistake. It's based on your
present patience and endurance.

The Enemy can use the memories of the past to
remind us of our sinful nature. He wants us to forget that
God spreads our sin as far as the east is from the west and
that we are the righteousness of God in Christ.

keep moving

What is something you can say to that voice the next
time it reminds you of your past?

improve your decisions

Trust in the LORD with all your heart, and do not rely on your
own understanding; in all your ways know him,
and he will make your paths straight.

PROVERBS 3:5-6 CSB

What makes a path straight? Is it that it's level, with no
bumps or potholes? How about curves? Can a straight
path have any twists and turns? If you think about it, the
thing that determines a straight path is your perspective.
If you're driving down a road with hills and turns and
ups and downs, you may look at it as crooked. But if you
concentrate on the next step on the path, the next moment
on the journey, that space is nice and smooth because it's
right in front of you.

That's how the Lord helps us. He doesn't remove
every obstacle in our way, but he gives us the perspective
to see the next best step. His wisdom leads us to the best
decisions possible.

The best way to move on from your past is to look
forward to your future. Find ways to make better choices. If
you keep running the same mistakes over and over through
your head, switch it by thinking about how to make good
choices just ahead. Keep your eyes on the next step rather
than constantly staring at your rearview mirror.

keep moving

What is one thing you do before making an
important decision?

no longer a victim

No, in all these things we are more than conquerors through him who loved us.

ROMANS 8:37 ESV

Many people refuse to take responsibility for themselves and instead delight in the false sense of security that blame brings. It's called the victim mindset. Our culture has been overtaken by victims.

What many of these victim-minded people do not realize is that taking responsibility affords them the luxury of healing. It takes courageous decision-making to experience that healing. The turmoil and circumstances in which some people live are of their own doing. These include those who cheated on their spouse, could not control their spending, or have an untamed tongue.

Others have been touched by evil and forced to live in a situation they did not create. They have been abused, abandoned, taken advantage of, or simply in the wrong place at the wrong time. The route to any of these circumstances is vastly different, but the way out can be the same. Declare today that you are more than a conqueror and leave the victim mindset behind.

keep moving

What is one way the victim mindset has held you back?

entitled to nothing

Because of God's great mercy to us I appeal to you:
Offer yourselves as a living sacrifice to God,
dedicated to his service and pleasing to him.
This is the true worship that you should offer.

ROMANS 12:1 GNT

What does God owe us? Nothing, really. Because of sin, we have earned eternal judgment. Because of faithlessness, we have earned a cold shoulder. But instead, God has freely given us everything we have. That's his great mercy on our lives. And it calls for a response of passionate service and not entitlement.

Someone may gain a sense of entitlement after receiving excessive gifts without any regard for the cost of the gift. Without understanding the cost, you have no idea how to properly steward the gift you have.

In the Old Testament, you brought something to the Lord. It was not something leftover but something that cost you something, such as the firstfruits of your crops or the firstborn of your herds. The offering meant something to you too. By understanding the cost, you were part of the process. Now, we offer ourselves up to God. We give what we most value—ourselves—because God gave what he most valued—Christ.

keep moving

What is one way you can be a living sacrifice to
God today?

reprogramming

Do not conform to the pattern of this world, but be
transformed by the renewing of your mind. Then you will
be able to test and approve what God's will is—his good,
pleasing and perfect will.

ROMANS 12:2 NIV

The inheritance we received from Adam and Eve, our sinful
nature, requires us to reprogram our brains. We should see
this ability as a gift more than anything else. Simply put, to
reprogram our brains to overcome our sinful nature takes
determination, but it trains us to keep going when we feel
like quitting.

Your brain likes to play tricks on you. It pulls up
negative memories of the past to keep you on lockdown.
It draws out destructive worries about present problems
to keep you from moving forward. It points to anxious
thoughts about an unsure future to get you to give up.
But a renewed mind is able to overcome these problems.
The reprogramming of your mind by the Holy Spirit can
literally rewrite the script in a way that provides clarity and
motivation to do his will.

The Holy Spirit is working with you. Keep going.
Don't give up. The power from him makes you more than a
conqueror.

keep moving

What is one thing you can do to reprogram your brain?

who came back?

Peter remembered that Jesus had said, "Before a rooster crows, you will say three times you don't know me." Then Peter went out and cried bitterly.

MATTHEW 26:75 CEV

Peter and Judas may be the two most famous disciples but for very different reasons. Peter was the leader of the disciples, whereas Judas was a schemer. Peter remained faithful to Jesus, founding his church on earth. Judas betrayed the Lord and sold him out to his enemies. Yet on the night Jesus was tried, both Peter and Judas denied him in their own way. Judas betrayed Jesus through his actions, Peter through his words. Their next moment defined their destiny.

You and I have encountered situations that have created turmoil in our lives. Some may be big, and others may be small. The mark of successfully learning your lesson is acknowledging the choices you have made and taking steps to make better decisions next time. You can make a choice like Peter to feel sorry and repent. Another choice— like the one Judas made—is to give up entirely.

It takes courage to show up when you know the circumstance hasn't been good. Peter grieved his mistakes and chose to rise above them. What will you do?

keep moving

Think of a time when you made a big mistake and came back from it.

faith expression

What is important is faith
expressing itself in love.

GALATIANS 5:6 NLT

There is a way to express our faith. We often think of faith
as an internal component: what we do in our heart, our
mind, our soul. But there is an outer expression of faith.
Not just the "leap of faith" you hear about. The actions
spurred on by true faith in God are expressed in a very
specific way: love.

What expressions of love come from our faith? Well,
when you think of other expressions of love—a kind note, a
text or phone call, a shared experience—those aren't exactly
what the Bible has in mind here. But they are close. In fact,
each of those can be an expression of love resulting from
faith. But true faith will show love by serving, by thinking
of others more than yourself, by not demanding your own
way. Romantic expressions of love can be manipulative,
doing something so you get a return. But faith expressions
of love are only about helping others. That's why they are so
motivating too. When you see how you are helping others,
you will want to do it even more.

keep moving

List a few ways that faith can express itself in love.

love indeed is love in deed

My children, our love should not be just words and talk;
it must be true love, which shows itself in action.

1 JOHN 3:18 GNT

Love is a verb. It's an action. It's not just a feeling, although a lot of times that's where it starts. But love always spurs us on to do something, to make something meaningful of our lives and the lives around us.

We often express love to each other in words. Make no mistake; it's really good to hear that someone loves us. But if they don't back it up with action, it's pretty hollow. If you've ever needed help and someone asked, "How can I help?" but then disappeared when you told them what you needed, you know this is the case. Now reverse it. What if you were able to help someone but you didn't? You said you would, but you failed to follow through. Is that real love?

Love indeed is love in deed. It has action behind it. And we all have the ability to do something with our love. That's why God puts dreams in your heart: to spur you to action. He loves his world, and he wants to do something about it. He has chosen you to act. So don't freeze up. It's time to move.

keep moving

What is one deed of love you can do today?

created for good works

We are God's handiwork, created in Christ Jesus to do good works, which God prepared in advance for us to do.

EPHESIANS 2:10 NIV

The problem with faith is that sometimes it can immobilize us. That sounds so odd, but it's true. If you have faith in a sovereign Lord, the one moving behind the scenes, then what's keeping you from saying, "You know what, if God wants this to happen, it'll happen. I don't need to do anything."

Your good works won't negate your faith. They didn't save you. You were saved for them. In fact, doing good works is a display of the faith you have in God.

God saved you for a purpose. That faith was the beginning of your journey, not the end. He has good works planned for you. Expressions of love and deeds of kindness for others. He planned this all out long ago too. He designed you with gifts and gave you a passion. Now, you have the opportunity to make something amazing happen. All it takes is putting that faith into gear and moving forward.

keep moving

What are some good works you've done as a result of your salvation?

what good is it?

You see, faith by itself isn't enough.
Unless it produces good deeds, it is dead and useless.

JAMES 2:17 NLT

Have you ever been holding your phone when suddenly it ran out of power? You end up holding a dark screen in your hand. It's useless. It can't do anything more than hold your papers down. It's the same with your faith. If it's not powered up, it'll take you nowhere.

What good is your faith if it doesn't do anything? If you don't act on it? If you refuse to move? If you're stuck in life, not serving others, not wanting to tell others about Jesus, not wanting to move on that dream you have, you may have faith in God, but it's just sitting on the shelf. There comes a time when you have to put your faith into action. Your works and your faith will then start to go hand in hand.

You didn't do anything to earn your salvation, and you can't do anything to keep it. But you can do something with it. By putting that faith into action, moving on your motive to love others more, serve others better, and climb ever higher, you will be displaying the gift that God has placed deep within you.

keep moving

What are some ways you can make your faith
work today?

let them see

"Make your light shine, so others will see the good you do
and will praise your Father in heaven."

MATTHEW 5:16 CEV

No one likes a show-off. It's not polite to brag. And you
definitely shouldn't try to make yourself look better than
others. But that doesn't mean you can't let others see your
good deeds. Often we try to hide our works behind a
curtain of modesty, afraid that the Lord won't bless us. But
this is the other side of that.

If you are humbly serving others, it's okay for the
public to know. Go ahead and post it on your social media,
giving God the glory. It's all right for people to know who
you are. In fact, it can be a good thing. Jesus told us that
one way we share the gospel is by what we do. When you
show the world your good deeds, they will praise your
Father in heaven, not you on earth.

Get moving today! Find some good deed to do and
let your light shine for others to see.

keep moving

List some reasons you don't like others seeing your
good deeds.

what's good?

He has shown you, O mortal, what is good. And what does the Lord require of you? To act justly and to love mercy and to walk humbly with your God.

MICAH 6:8 NIV

We might get stuck because we just don't know what to do next. In the middle of chasing after that dream God has placed in our hearts, we feel like we're in between assignments. We've done all that we know to do. We're just waiting for God to show us the next step. What if there were some way to keep momentum?

God has shown us exactly what we should do. He has given us a list of the good that we can do. First, we should act justly. Treat others with respect. Don't play favorites. When you see anyone in need, regardless of who they are, make a point to help out. Next, love mercy. Forgive quickly and don't hold a grudge. Finally, walk humbly. Worship your Lord by putting others before yourself. There is so much power in humility. It can ignite a passion that will send you into a bright future.

keep moving

List three ways you can practice these three good things.

keep the faith

I have fought the good fight.
I have completed the race.
I have kept the faith.

2 TIMOTHY 4:7 GW

At the end of your life, what do you want to see when you look back? Would you in that moment want to spend time thinking of all the bad you've done, the mistakes you've made, or the wrongs you've committed? Of course not! Fill your life with fruitful acts and faithful devotion and you'll have a scrapbook full of great things to remember.

There is a fight ahead. It's a battle for your very soul. Fight it in a way that brings honor to God and joy to your soul. There is a race you're a part of. You're not in competition with others, but you are tasked with running well. Don't get sidetracked. Stay on pace.

You have a path to keep to. And faith is the key. If you remain faithful to God and rekindle the faith you have in God, then God will keep his promise to you. All the things you've always hoped for are within reach. Don't give up! Don't give out! It's not too long now. Keep the faith.

keep moving

Make a list of good things you've accomplished in life so far.

september

grace

goodness gracious

"May the LORD smile on you
and be gracious to you."

NUMBERS 6:25 NLT

God's graciousness to you is incomparable. It's amazing!
It's fantastic! You start to run out of adjectives when you
realize what it really means. God's grace is more than just
a blessing someone says to you after you sneeze. It's more
than a quick prayer you speak over dinner too.

Grace is a gift. That's the literal translation of the
word *grace*. But it's more than that. It's the very act of giving
on the part of God—who has everything—to us on the
other end—who have nothing of our own.

When we call out for God's grace, we first have to
recognize that we cannot do this thing called life all by
ourselves. We need help. We need God's help. Not just a
hand or a boost. But the very breath we take in to start our
blood flowing is the beginning of God's grace. The life you
have is an indication that you need God.

Notice this blessing asks that God would smile on
us. That means he turns his face to you. He recognizes and
regards you. He is happy with you. He doesn't pity you. He's
not disappointed in you. He loves you so much that he is
excited about showering you with grace. So why not let him?

keep moving

What grace have you already received from God today?

he won't hold back

The LORD God is a sun and shield. The LORD grants favor and honor. He does not hold back any blessing from those who live innocently.

PSALM 84:11 GW

Admit it. Sometimes you hold back. Maybe you're in charge of scooping out the ice cream for everyone else, and you hold back on how much you give them…until it gets to you. It's okay. It's natural to want more than you give others. But it's supernatural to give out as much as you can to everyone you can. That's how God acts toward us.

God won't hold back. He doesn't keep some grace, gift, or blessing in reserve for a rainy day. He won't wait until you've earned it. Even in the middle of your worst day, he is willing to shower you with grace. Even in the midst of your struggles, he turns on the faucet. He's ready and able to give you all you need.

Another translation of this verse says, "The LORD will withhold no good thing" (NLT). If it's good, it's God, and it comes from God. Grace is the process of moving good stuff into your life. But God is in love with the idea of overflowing grace in everyone's life.

keep moving

Why do you think God refuses to hold back on his grace?

saved by grace

You are saved by grace through faith,
and this is not from yourselves; it is God's gift.

EPHESIANS 2:8 CSB

The rules were written long ago to help us live a life worthy of God's calling. The only problem was that the standard was just too high. No one could ever fulfill every single point of the law every single day. So something had to be done. The law could be rewritten. Or it could be fulfilled. God chose the second one.

You do not have to earn your salvation. All you have to do is believe in Jesus—that's the faith part of the equation. You trust in God fully for salvation, meaning you aren't really doing anything at all. And then God gives you salvation—that's the grace part of the equation.

Salvation is a gift God means for you to share though. In retelling the story of your own faith journey, you are strengthening others' walk with God. In leading others to Christ, you are exercising the gifts he has given you. In discipling other believers, you are living out one aspect of that dream God has placed in your heart. Grace is not meant to be a cover-up for the problems of our past; it's meant to be the fuel for the challenges in our future.

keep moving

Have you ever considered salvation as a reward for
your hard work?

justified by grace

All are justified freely by his grace
through the redemption that came by Christ Jesus.

ROMANS 3:24 NIV

God saves you by his grace and then justifies you by his grace. But wait! Aren't they the same thing? Not really. Salvation and justification are definitely related, but they describe different aspects of the same thing. First, salvation is the forgiveness of sins in your past. You are saved from a pointless life. You are saved from the consequences of sin. You are saved from an eternity apart from God. All those are promised to you at salvation.

Second, justification is the act of making you righteous. At the moment you believe, Jesus begins the work of changing your life. However, you are completely changed in an instant. God writes your name in his Book. You are fully accepted into his family. Those things don't happen over time but at one time.

Neither of those things is acquired through hard work. They are freely given. But they are also given so that you will work hard to show the world how great God is. That's part of the dream he has placed in your heart. If you are saved and justified, then you are ready to start chasing that dream down.

keep moving

How have you seen a difference in your life before
and after salvation?

be gracious

Hear, O LORD, when I cry aloud;
be gracious to me and answer me!

PSALM 27:7 ESV

What do you need? Like, right now what is the most pressing thing on your agenda, the most stressing lack in your life, or the most oppressing burden you have? In this moment, cry out to the Lord and ask him for it. We call that prayer, but it's also grace.

To cry out to God first puts us in the back seat. We are saying that we cannot control what is happening. We no longer have enough power to solve this. We need God! What a freeing thing to say. We often get stuck because we don't think we can take one more step. And that's true. It's only by the grace of God that we can.

That's the next thing that crying out to God does. It puts him in the driver's seat. Asking for God to be gracious to us is an indication that we won't go until he says so. He is the one calling the shots, and he is the one holding the wheel. Don't try to take it back from him. Don't give him your plans and ask him to bless them. Turn the playbook completely over to him and allow his wisdom and strength to guide you.

keep moving

Take a moment to ask God for grace in all areas of your life.

grace for grace

Of his fulness we all received,
and grace for grace.

JOHN 1:16 ASV

What happens if you run out of gas? You have to go on foot to get more and then fill your tank back up. What happens if your phone dies? You have to plug it back in and wait for a new charge. What happens if you don't have enough milk? You have to leave the house to pick up more.

What happens if you run out of grace? Trick question! You never run out. Once God gives you grace, he doesn't step back to see what you do with it. He's not judging you to make sure you're deserving. He lines up more grace for you. He has a fullness, so full that there's more than enough for each of us for all time. So why would he ever not want to shower you with grace?

Maybe if you mess up, right? That's a good reason to withhold grace. Let's get back to living right, and then he'll give us some more. No, that's not how it works. In fact, if you do sin, he will give you even more grace. Where sin abounds, grace abounds even more (see Romans 5:20). So the good news is that you don't have to wait or try to earn extra grace. All you have to do is keep moving in his ever-flowing grace.

keep moving

Have you ever felt like you needed to earn God's favor?

we're all saved the same way

"We believe that we are all saved the same way,
by the undeserved grace of the Lord Jesus."

ACTS 15:11 NLT

We each have our own story of how we came to Jesus. Maybe it happened at church or over at a friend's house. You might have had a bunch of questions you needed answered first, or it could have been a spur of the moment thing. Some have a particular date and even time when they got saved. Others point to a season of talking with God that led to salvation. Regardless of how different our individual stories are, we all came to Jesus the same way—through grace.

The story in Acts 15 is an interesting one. Jesus, being a Jew, had sent Jewish followers to talk to other Jews about his plan of salvation. Once non-Jews (called gentiles) heard about this, they wanted in on it too. Some Jewish people had a problem with that. They wanted to draw up some extra rules to make sure the gentiles were ready to become Christians. But others saw no issue at all. After all, we all come to Jesus the same way—through grace. And we all move on in life the same way with that same grace.

keep moving

Have you ever thought that another believer should have to earn their salvation even though you didn't have to?

grace and truth

We saw his true glory, the glory of the only Son of the Father. From him the complete gifts of undeserved grace and truth have come down to us.

JOHN 1:14 CEV

Flip a coin. It's either heads or tails. We use this analogy to explain how two seemingly opposite ideas can be part of the same principle. Like sweet and sour. Or like saving and spending. We say it's two sides of the same coin.

Grace and truth are two sides of the same coin. It's all about salvation and how we live that out in Christ. So on one hand, you have grace. God has given us everything we need. We don't do a thing. But on the other hand, you have truth. Truth hurts sometimes. So maybe this means we have to set a standard to live by or else.

But that's not really accurate. The thing is that truth and grace are never opposed to each other. They aren't opposite ends of the same argument. They are complementary of one another. The truth is that we can't do it on our own. The grace is that God can and will. The truth is that Jesus did it all. The grace is that all we have to do is ask. Don't get stuck in the middle of truth and grace. Move through life with both in hand.

keep moving

How do you see grace and truth operating in your life?

greater than your greatest sin

There is no comparison between [God's] gift and [Adam's] failure. If humanity died as the result of one person's failure, it is certainly true that God's kindness and the gift given through the kindness of one person, Jesus Christ, have been showered on humanity.

ROMANS 5:15 GW

We all bear the mark of Adam on our lives. Because of what he and Eve did in the garden, we are cursed with a sin nature. The gift Adam gave to humanity is mistake and error. We must overcome it, but we can't on our own. That's where God's gift comes in.

Adam's failure was pretty big. After all, every single person who has ever lived has suffered from it. Think about that—over eight billion people today are affected by Adam's sin in some form or another. That's a lot! So what was God going to do about it? He showered all humanity with his grace. He sent his Son to die for us. He rescued us from our troubles. He gave us something remarkable in his will and design. He made you something greater than you could be by giving you something greater than the sin that holds you back. So hold on to his grace and get going into a bright future.

keep moving

Do you consider yourself blessed?

give us freedom

Sin is no longer your master,
for you no longer live under the requirements of the law.
Instead, you live under the freedom of God's grace.

ROMANS 6:14 NLT

Being stuck in life is the exact opposite of freedom. You are locked in by your failure, your past, your own selfishness, or your poor self-esteem. You can't seem to get any space to move in life. You are going nowhere fast. What do you need?

Shaking off the sins that hold us down would help. What if you had never sinned a day in your life? Do you think you would be further along than you are right now? Maybe, but it doesn't matter because all of us have sinned at some point in life. The best we can do is ask God to forgive us and unchain us.

Grace is freedom. It breaks the chains that hold us back. It opens the door that feels closed. It removes the walls that have us closed in. When you have the grace of God in your life, sin no longer has control over you. It's not calling the shots or making you do what you don't want to. You'll still be tempted, but you won't be dragged under every day. Instead, you can walk proudly into the dream God has planted in your heart.

keep moving

What is one way that God has freed you from
your past?

meant to live

God's readiness to give and forgive is now public.
Salvation's available for everyone! We're being shown how
to turn our backs on a godless, indulgent life, and how to
take on a God-filled, God-honoring life.

TITUS 2:11-14 MSG

What does God's grace do? I'm not asking what it does for
us. That's pretty evident. It saves us. It brings us into right
relationship with God. It makes us righteous and grants us
freedom. But it also works in our lives. How? It shows us
how to live.

We were not meant to live lives of sinfulness and
selfishness. Your body was not designed for sinful living.
Your soul was not knitted together by God to withstand
the weathering of sin. Sinfulness is a foreign body in our
lives. Grace is like the antidote, not only clearing out the
infection but helping us build an immunity to future sins.

When your flesh desires to sin, where do you go?
Do you rely on your own self-control and ability to pull
yourself out of the temptation? Or do you look for the
escape? God has shown you how to flee sinful lusts, and
that path is a path of grace. You will be continually stuck if
you do not learn to live the way God means for you to live.

keep moving

What are some habits or hang-ups that have
weighed you down?

grow in grace

Grow in the grace and knowledge of our Lord and Savior Jesus Christ. To him be glory both now and forever! Amen.

2 PETER 3:18 NIV

How much grace do you have? Did you know you can grow in grace? God does not give a set amount. He loves to pour it out over and over again. And the grace you do have on hand will continue to grow. When you nourish it and foster it, you will begin to see more and more grace.

That's because grace is expandable. It's not available for only one area of your life. It might seem that grace is only for the Sundays of our weeks. Or that grace is only for our quiet times with God when we are reading our Bible or praying. But once we get to work, that's not a grace area.

But it is! God wants us to give his grace room to grow. He likes to spread his grace out and cover so much of your life. So let it. Give it plenty of space to move between you and other people so that your relationships are seasoned with love. Let grace out in times where you don't really think of it, like in a meeting or on the phone. Maybe God wants you to show his grace where you least expect. You never know when grace will get a growth spurt.

keep moving

Have you ever felt grace in a place you didn't expect?

i am what i am

By the grace of God I am what I am,
and his grace toward me was not in vain.

1 Corinthians 15:10 esv

Grace takes an active role in shaping who you are. Sin may corrupt your natural design, but God has his sights set on renovating you. He knows what he has put in you, and he wants to see it come out. If sin is stopping that, then grace will abound to match it and surpass it. You are what you are because of God's grace. It moves in your life, activating your strengths and speeding you along.

No one can truly fulfill God's dream for their lives without grace. That's because we are stuck in a shell of our old selves without it. We will be bogged down with doubt or question who we are. But when we have grace and truly understand it, we begin to see ourselves the way God does. And we can fully be who we are. That way, we are ready to move forward with God's strength. God does not give his grace to you in vain. It's working right now to make you a better version than your old self.

keep moving

How has God's grace already started working on you?

full of grace

Stephen, a man full of God's grace and power,
performed amazing miracles and signs among the people.

ACTS 6:8 NLT

There have been many people in the Bible who are famous.
We know their stories well. Some of them have books
that bear their name, like Jonah and Joshua and John.
For others, their names are repeated again and again, like
Moses and Abraham. But then there are those who feel like
background characters. We may get a chapter or two of
their story, but outside of that, we don't really know much.
One such person is Stephen.

The disciples chose Stephen to help in the ministry
to widows. That is such an important part of the work of
the church. Everyone saw something in Stephen that led
them to put him in charge. Maybe he was really good with
logistics, or perhaps he had great people skills. We don't
know. What we do know is that he was full of grace. And
that grace simply amplified his God-given talents, amplified
them so much that he was performing miracles. What
kind? Again, we're not sure. They could have been healings
and casting out demons. Maybe he was able to get two
enemies to sit down and talk it over; that's often a miracle
in itself. Whatever those miracles were, they were all due to
the fullness of God's grace in Stephen's life.

keep moving

How might you go about seeking to be full of
God's grace?

everyone can see

The grace of God has appeared that offers salvation to all people.

TITUS 2:11 NIV

God's grace doesn't hide. It shows up in all areas of life and on all occasions. Most of all, it shows up at the point of salvation. In fact, that's why it appears to every person.

One event in which we think of God's grace appearing is when Jesus was on the cross. The Bible tells us that his enemies made a public spectacle of Jesus. That might have been by design. Seeing the pain and suffering our Savior went through reminds us that his grace is even greater than we could imagine.

Another way that God's grace appears to us is through his people. Grace can overlook a problem or a sin. Grace can watch out for those who need help. Grace can bring friends together. All that is grace appearing through the work of believers in the real world. And as his grace appears, it brings along with it the hope of salvation. While you are pursuing your goals, think of how God's grace is working in that moment to shine the light of salvation to everyone you bump into.

keep moving

How are you making God's grace evident to those around you?

saved and called

He has saved us and called us to a holy life—
not because of anything we have done
but because of his own purpose and grace.

2 TIMOTHY 1:9 NIV

God's salvation was not the end of his work in your life. It was just the beginning. It's sad to think that there are those who believe all they need to do is say yes to Jesus in their minds. Like after checking a box on a card, they stop thinking about that part of their life. Finished. Over. Now they've punched their ticket to heaven. What else could there be?

But God's grace is not just for salvation alone. He saved you, and he called you. He rescued you for something great. He pulled you from the clutches of the Enemy so you could keep running in life. He woke you from a nightmare existence to set you on the path toward your dream.

If you stopped moving forward after you came to Jesus, now is the time to start moving again. Salvation is not the end of your journey; it's the beginning of the next. The altar of the church is not a finish line but a starting line. It's where new life begins. So don't stop. Keep going.

keep moving

What has God called you to do?

sufficient

"My grace is all you need, for my power is greatest when you are weak." I am most happy, then, to be proud of my weaknesses, in order to feel the protection of Christ's power over me.

2 CORINTHIANS 12:9 GNT

Have you ever prayed for something, and you just didn't feel like you got an answer? Or at least you didn't get the answer you wanted. That happened to Paul. He prayed at least three times for God to remove from his life a certain situation that was causing him weakness. Instead, God told him that he wasn't going to do it. Maybe it was God saying that this was best for Paul, or perhaps there was a greater, unseen reason that God was not going to do what Paul wanted him to do.

God did what was best for Paul. Paul's life after being told no was better than before. Why? Because of God's grace. The kindness and mercy he provided Paul after that moment were sufficient for all his needs. And whatever weakness Paul felt, God was going to fill in the gaps with his own power. He was going to be strong for Paul, and Paul didn't have to worry about it. Paul was able to keep moving forward, not because of answered prayer but because of God's grace in the midst of persistent problems.

keep moving

Think of a problem you have in life. How can God's grace provide strength in your weakness?

all you need

God is able to make every grace overflow to you,
so that in every way, always having everything you need,
you may excel in every good work.

2 CORINTHIANS 9:8 CSB

Have you ever heard about the principle of a scarcity mindset? It's the feeling that you'll never have enough. You could have this feeling concerning money, time, connections, status, or security. If you experience scarcity regarding connection, you feel lonely. If you think about scarcity when it comes to employment, you will feel stuck in a dead-end job. If your mind is made up that you never have good opportunities, you may never get moving in life.

The fact of the matter is that no one should have a scarcity mindset because everyone is rich in the grace of God. Through his great mercies and kindness, we have all we need. He does not hold back on anything that will help us. In fact, he offers it to us in abundance. The only thing that is keeping us from moving forward and taking hold of what God wants for us is our own way of thinking. Let's shift from a scarcity mindset to a gracious mindset, one set on the abundance of God's blessings in our lives.

keep moving

What is an area in your life in which you've had a scarcity mindset?

abundance

Grace and peace be yours in abundance through
the knowledge of God and of Jesus our Lord.

2 Peter 1:2 niv

What does abundance mean to you? Is it more than
enough or just more than you have? We can get tricked into
thinking that success is a level above where we are. It is said
that when a reporter asked John D. Rockefeller, famous
business leader and once the richest man in the world,
"How much money is enough money?" Rockefeller replied,
"Just a little bit more."

God does not want us to keep striving in life, chasing
after an extra dollar, a bigger circle of friends, a higher level
of influence. He wants us running on his grace. He wants
us to know that we never need to reach for just a little bit
more because all that we have is more than we need. It's
abundance.

Abundance means you have enough left over. Not
that you keep gaining more. Tap into the abundant grace
and peace God gives you and share this gift with those
around you. Satisfaction won't be marked by a number but
by a feeling of ever-expanding grace.

keep moving

When was the last time you really felt like you
had enough?

grace wins

When it's sin versus grace, grace wins hands down. All sin can do is threaten us with death, and that's the end of it. Grace, because God is putting everything together again through the Messiah, invites us into life—a life that goes on and on and on, world without end.

ROMANS 5:20-21 MSG

What's the score in your life? How often have you let sin win? How many times have you felt like you let God down? You gave in to temptation. You said what you shouldn't have said. You gave up on a dream.

Do you want to know the score? It's 1–0. Grace has won. Grace always wins! No matter how beaten up you are, how guilty your past tries to make you think you are, or how shameful your situation gets you feeling, you can share the truth of the matter with others. Grace is winning. Grace will win. Grace always does. That's because grace is bigger than sin.

Every time you sin, you don't move back to square one. Sin doesn't gain an edge on you. Why? Because every time you sin, God's grace increases in your life. You are not moving further away from God's goal. You are simply slowing down or stopping. Remove the sin, repent of your mistakes, and move forward knowing that God's grace is winning in your life.

keep moving

What is your first response when you feel guilty?

strengthened by grace

You then, my child, be strengthened
by the grace that is in Christ Jesus.

2 Timothy 2:1 esv

Do you ever feel weak, worn out, or even run over? Like life is taking it out on you personally. You've done all you can to make it through or get ahead, but you constantly feel beaten down and blown back. What you'd like to see is a bit of progress. What you get is heartache and frustration.

It's okay to feel this way sometimes. The problem comes when this feeling gets you stuck. You give up and don't want to move forward. It may be because you don't think you have the strength to move forward. You might not. But God does.

His grace is what strengthens you. Not a new workout or better sleep, although those can give you physical strength. But soul strength comes from the grace of God. Coming to him for that gift of life-giving power could be the one thing you need to get ahead in life.

keep moving

Think of a time when you felt like giving up but didn't.

a great approach

Let us approach the throne of grace with boldness,
so that we may receive mercy and find grace
to help us in time of need.

HEBREWS 4:16 CSB

The throne of grace is a spiritual reality. For centuries it was represented by a physical marker, known as the ark of the covenant, behind the temple veil in the holy of holies. Only the high priest was allowed to approach, and even then, he could only once a year. All others were kept out, excluded.

But then came the cross. While Jesus was suffering and dying, inside the temple something amazing happened. God reached down and tore the curtain in two, symbolizing that all have access to him. Now we can boldly approach his throne.

What does the throne offer? Grace. We approach not because we are worthy or because we have the right credentials. Not because of our bloodline or because of who we know. But because we are already accepted. We approach that throne by means of God's grace. And we approach that throne to receive more grace. The grace upon grace is what keeps us moving forward.

keep moving

What are some ways you can confidently approach God's throne?

bankrupt

You know the generous grace of our Lord Jesus Christ.
Though he was rich, yet for your sakes he became poor,
so that by his poverty he could make you rich.

2 CORINTHIANS 8:9 NLT

How much would you give to help a friend? Someone is
in dire need of your assistance, and only you can step in to
stop whatever it is that is keeping them back. Maybe it's a
medical condition or a debt that is overwhelming. It could
be an emotional trauma. Let's say that it's a life-and-death
situation, but it will bankrupt you to help them out. Would
you do it?

You probably would if it were a close friend or
relative. For a stranger, probably not. With Jesus, he did just
that so that you could have freedom from your sins. God
bankrupted heaven to make you rich. He gave up the most
valuable thing in the heavenlies—his Son—so that you
could have a new life. And he did it gladly! That's because
his grace is so powerful. And it means so much to us. Let's
thank him for bankrupting heaven by living a rich and full
life, unstuck from the sin that has held us back.

keep moving

Make a list of the riches you've received from God.

soul stewardship

As each one has received a gift, minister it to one another, as good stewards of the manifold grace of God.

1 PETER 4:10 NKJV

Good financial stewards keep track of their expenses and make the most of their investments. Good stewards of talent will use their gifts to benefit others. But what of soul stewardship? How do we steward God's grace?

To steward means to manage or oversee something that you do not own but have been given charge over. God has given you grace. He placed no prerequisites on it. He did not force you to sign a document. God freely gave you his grace. But now that you have received it, you have some responsibilities. What you do with the grace God gives you will determine whether you stay where you are or move out into God's plan for your life.

Notice that the grace is not singular but "manifold." That means it covers every aspect of your life. That's why it's so important to steward it. Take care of your grace by determining to live a holy life. Oversee his grace by looking out for others in need of grace. Steward your grace by sharing your grace with those who don't know the Lord. That way you will live a full life while also helping others realize their own God-given dreams.

keep moving

What is one way you can engage in soul stewardship today?

mercy

"Blessed are the merciful,
for they will be shown mercy."

MATTHEW 5:7 NIV

Mercy is the act of showing grace. It's giving something to someone who doesn't deserve it. Another way to think of mercy is to not give someone what they deserve. To have mercy on a prisoner on death row means the government would commute their sentence to life without parole, sparing the prisoner's life. In other words, the prisoner does not receive the penalty they deserve.

There will be people in your life who deserve to be punished. They may have hurt you, or worse, they hurt someone you're close to. They have not earned forgiveness. They shouldn't get it. But they do. That's what mercy is.

When we show others mercy, we open ourselves up to blessing. Why? Because all of us deserve punishment for some wrong. We deserve to be judged for holding a grudge or saying something bad or breaking God's commandments. Instead, God is merciful to us. When we show mercy to others, he will bless us with even more mercy. No longer locked in our past, forgiving others will give us motivation to move forward.

keep moving

Look for a way to show mercy to someone today.

an eye for value

Recognize the value of every person and continually show love to every believer. Live your lives with great reverence and in holy awe of God.

1 PETER 2:17 TPT

Do you have an eye for value? You read labels, knowing which ingredients are high-quality. You pay attention to trends, picking up on the latest fashions. You can tell when a product is made better than another. You know what kind of car will last longer, what type of tech will have fewer bugs, which housebuilder is more reliable. But do you have an eye for value when it comes to other people?

Often we refuse to show mercy to others or give them grace for their mistakes or shortcomings because we just don't see a need for it. After all, they were in the wrong. But when you recognize the value of other people, you are more likely to give them grace just as God showed you mercy because he saw great value in you. If he had not, then he wouldn't have put that dream in your heart. When you recognize the value of other people, you will love them and care for them. Not because you are obligated to but because you are acting in godliness. And that godliness is what will keep you unstuck in life.

keep moving

Who is someone you have devalued in life? How can you recognize their value?

just like you

"Treat others just as you want to be treated."

LUKE 6:31 CEV

When it comes to our mistakes, we want grace. When it comes to another person's problems, we want justice. But that mindset is actually the opposite of justice. You see, the Hebrew word for "justice" is the exact same as the root word for "righteousness." And no one is more just and righteous than God. So what does he do to that person whom you think deserves judgment? He holds off. He shows them grace. And you should too.

The simple reason is that we should treat others the way we want to be treated. Why? One practical reason is that others will treat us how we want to be treated if we make the first move. Another way to think about this is that God will show us mercy when we show mercy to others. But there may be yet another way of looking at this verse.

Treat others just like you want to be treated. Just like you. That's the important part because the person who has offended you is just like you. How? Because you have surely offended someone in life. So when you treat someone just like you want to be treated, you're treating them fairly because they are just like you.

keep moving

Who is someone you need to treat "just as you want to be treated"?

first forgive

Make allowance for each other's faults, and forgive anyone who offends you. Remember, the Lord forgave you, so you must forgive others.

COLOSSIANS 3:13 NLT

Real talk: What did you do to earn your salvation? Nothing. In fact, you didn't even ask for it. Sure, when you got saved, you asked God to forgive you. But Jesus already won that forgiveness on the cross and made it available to everyone long before you were born. You weren't around in time to ask Jesus to die for you. He did it first before you could ask.

With that in mind, think about the last grudge you held. You were probably waiting for the other person to make the first move. "If they ask forgiveness, then I'll forgive them. But I can't do that before then." That's actually not how it works. If you wait for the other person to make the first move, you'll be stuck in neutral. And neutral goes nowhere. Instead, be the first to forgive.

God was the first to forgive you. And his forgiveness is better than yours. He is able to forgive so much more than you are able to. Because of his forgiveness, you are even able to forgive others. So make the first move, get out of neutral, and get moving into your destiny.

keep moving

Is there anyone in your life whom you are waiting to forgive?

don't jump

Don't jump to conclusions—there may be a perfectly good explanation for what you just saw.

PROVERBS 25:8 MSG

When someone hurts you, what's your first response? Is it to blame them or yourself for what happened? Maybe you get angry and lash out. Whatever that first response is, it may determine how quickly you get unstuck and start moving forward again. If you jump to conclusions without knowing all the details, you may be operating on a false belief. And that will affect every step you take after that.

There is a difference between an explanation and an excuse. An excuse is a reason someone gives for you to ignore a behavior that they don't take any responsibility for. On the other hand, an explanation is a reason someone gives for a certain behavior with a commitment to do better next time. Keep your ears open for an explanation. Learn to actively listen to others as they tell you why they acted the way they did. Perhaps they, too, were relying on a false belief. Now you have the chance to correct two wrongs.

When you jump to conclusions, you may also be jumping off God's path for your life. Keeping your eyes on Jesus will keep you from jumping someplace you shouldn't.

keep moving

Think of a time you jumped to a conclusion and then later learned the truth.

life isn't over until...

I don't care what happens to me, as long as I finish the work
the Lord Jesus gave me to do. And this work is to tell the
good news about God's gift of undeserved grace.

ACTS 20:24 CEV

These are the words of Paul. He spent a lot of time thinking
about grace. He also spent a lot of time writing and talking
about grace. That may be because the first half of his life
was pretty absent of grace. He was more of a judgment-
first type of person. He was quick to condemn and slow
to forgive. Later in life, after encountering the risen Lord,
he changed his tune. After that, he was committed to one
thing. His life wasn't over until he had told everyone he
could about God's grace.

What will you decide to do with your life? You
could commit to earning as much money as you can before
retirement. You might even build your own personal
empire. Maybe you're devoted to your family or friends. But
what about God's grace? What are you doing with it? Your
life is not over until you tell everyone you can about him.
Why not start today?

keep moving

Think of one person you can share the grace of God
with today.

october

spiritual warfare

unearthly

Our struggle is not against flesh and blood, but against the rulers, against the authorities, against the powers of this dark world and against the spiritual forces of evil in the heavenly realms.

EPHESIANS 6:12 NIV

Here is some good news and bad news for you. The bad news first. You are under attack. The enemies in the spiritual realm are dark and evil. They have authority over certain situations in your life, and they have been tasked with making your life a living hell. They come from the darkest corners of this world, and they want to drag you back with them.

The good news is there is an unearthly power that wants to set you free. God wants to rescue you from this present darkness. He has the authority to do it too. Through his flesh and blood, you can overcome anything in life, including those powers that are not flesh and blood.

The first stage of spiritual warfare is acceptance. Accept that there are things you don't understand, that you can't explain. They are not visible to the human eye or observable by scientific means. They are out there, and they influence us. But we are completely covered by Jesus' blood, so we have nothing to fear.

keep moving

Do you find it hard or easy to accept that there is a spiritual realm?

not unaware

I don't want Satan to outwit us.
After all, we are not ignorant about Satan's scheming.

2 Corinthians 2:11 GW

There are usually two camps when it comes to spiritual warfare. The first camp is gung ho. They are ready to learn. They search out every Scripture passage and listen to every testimony about the spiritual realm. On the other end, you have those who are a bit leery of it. They don't necessarily think spiritual warfare doesn't exist; they just don't want to make a big deal about it. In the middle are those who are aware. That's where God wants us to be because he knows that if we are ignorant of the Enemy's schemes, we are bound to fall for them.

When you go on vacation, you want to know about the possibility of pickpockets. If you drive down a road, you want to know about the hazards ahead. There are major obstacles in the life God has laid out for you. He has not removed them, but he wants you to be aware of them. As we walk not unaware of the strategies of the Enemy, we are less likely to fall into a trap or get stuck somewhere.

keep moving

On a scale of one to ten, with one being not very and ten being very much, how would you rate your perception of the spiritual realm?

where we stand

He has delivered us from the domain of darkness and transferred us to the kingdom of his beloved Son.

COLOSSIANS 1:13 ESV

You were under the devil's control. You were answerable to his kingdom. That is until you got saved. Once you accept Jesus Christ as Lord of your life, your citizenship switched. You are no longer captive to the Enemy. You are secured in God's kingdom.

The image you can get in your mind is that of a kidnapping victim, say, in the Middle Ages. A knight comes riding into the castle, setting the captives free. But the released prisoners do not leave on their own. That same valiant knight takes them with him home to his castle and his father. That's exactly what is going on in the spiritual realm every time someone gets saved.

You are not on shaky ground as a believer. Your feet are on solid ground. The Enemy would have you believe otherwise. He wants you to doubt your salvation and wonder if you are really safe. Why? Because he knows that fear will lock you up and freeze you in place. Instead, you are free to move because you are rescued by Christ.

keep moving

Do you ever think that maybe you have not been rescued, that you are still under the Enemy's control? What do you do to convince yourself it's not true?

the overcomer

"I have told you these things, so that in me you may have peace. In this world you will have trouble. But take heart! I have overcome the world."

JOHN 16:33 NIV

God has promised us much about this world. He promised that he would rescue us from the power of this world. He promised he would return for us one day. He promised to be with us at all times. He promised that we could ask him anything in his name and he would do it. He also promised us trouble.

Wait, what? Are you thinking, *You really mean he promised that we would have tough times? Surely, he's able to erase all that bad stuff. Can't he just make it so that life is easier for us now?*

Well, he actually promised us two things. First, that we would have trouble. But second, that he has overcome the world. Notice he didn't say, "*You* have overcome the world." He said that the world may just be a bit bigger than we are. But that's okay because we follow the Overcomer. And where he has gone, we can go too. So know that no matter what happens in life, as long as we keep our eye on the Overcomer, we will be safe.

keep moving

What does it mean to you that Jesus has overcome the world?

strong and mighty?

He said to me, "This is the word of the LORD to Zerubbabel: 'Not by might nor by power, but by my Spirit,' says the LORD Almighty."

ZECHARIAH 4:6 NIV

What's the biggest trophy you own? Whatever that trophy is, it represents something you accomplished. You were strong and mighty. You outlasted others to be the best.

But in the spiritual realm, that trophy doesn't mean much. The Enemy doesn't care that you were good at shot put or that you were talented in dance. He is coming for you. You'll need more than just a shiny piece of metal and plastic to keep him off.

When the nation of Israel felt their most vulnerable, God reassured the Israelites that they were safe. Zerubbabel wasn't a very distinguished governor or mighty warrior. But he was humble. And God answered his humility by raising him up to be a great leader. And then he surrounded Zerubbabel with his Holy Spirit to protect him. The Lord is doing the same for you today. If you just believe him, he will protect you. And he will arm you for the fight of your life so that you can chase after the goal he has set before you.

keep moving

How does God give you strength today through his Holy Spirit?

our authority

"Look, I have given you the authority to trample on snakes and scorpions and over all the power of the enemy; nothing at all will harm you."

LUKE 10:19 CSB

No one really likes snakes and scorpions. Some may say they do, but it's really just a fascination. Snakes are cold-blooded. They slither on the ground. They have huge fangs. Scorpions have stingers on the ends of their tails, ready to strike.

But it's what snakes and scorpions represent that's the real problem. All throughout Scripture, they are symbols of evil, of deceit and lies, of the Enemy. And Jesus said, "I have given you the authority to trample on snakes and scorpions."

Where does our authority come from? Jesus. On the cross is where he wrestled control of the dark spiritual realms. In a sense, he put his foot on the neck of Satan and invites us to do the same.

That's our right. The devil will tell you otherwise. But you do have authority in this life over dark thoughts and demonic attacks. Let no one tell you differently. And don't get stuck in fear over snakes and scorpions, in evil and lies. You have authority.

keep moving

Make a list of things you have authority over in life through Jesus Christ.

seven ways to victory

"The LORD will conquer your enemies when they attack you. They will attack you from one direction, but they will scatter from you in seven!"

DEUTERONOMY 28:7 NLT

How strong are you really? How much can you lift? Know any martial arts? How about firearms? How many do you own? Unfortunately, none of that will help you in the fight with the Enemy over your soul. But that doesn't matter either because God has already won the victory. He has conquered your Enemy. He has settled the battle. You may still be under attack, but he will fight for you.

It's great to have the protection of someone bigger than you. You feel invincible even if you really aren't. You have this incredible freedom to go anywhere you want and do anything you want. You have no reason to stay stuck where you are. Just picture the Enemy scattering seven different ways while you walk into the room. That's how complete your victory is. There is nothing that can stop you because you have God on your side.

keep moving

What could you do today knowing that God is fighting for you?

hearing God

You will hear a voice behind you saying, "This is the way. Follow it, whether it turns to the right or to the left."

ISAIAH 30:21 GW

God breaks through our physical realm from the spiritual realm in very real ways. The most common way is through his voice. We often think that his voice is audible, out loud. But it's not always. Most of the time it's a still, small voice within. Our heart listens to his heart. Our spirit hears his Spirit. Our mind is attuned to his mind. That's what it means to hear God.

He does not have a speaking problem; we have a listening problem. It's hard to hear God's voice not because of his tone or his volume but because of our inattention. We don't hear God sometimes because we're not asking him to speak. All you need to do is ask and then wait. God responds to simple prayers. There is not some super-spiritual formula or some special preparation to go through. He doesn't speak to just these people and not those. He will talk to all his children. And as children, when we patiently wait for his voice, we will not just hear but be encouraged. We will go from stuck to fully alive and thriving. So listen up and hear him today.

keep moving

What are some ways you can attune your spirit to hear God's Spirit?

set the atmosphere

Remember what it says: "Today when you hear his voice, don't harden your hearts as Israel did when they rebelled."

HEBREWS 3:15 NLT

If we ask the Lord to speak and we still don't hear, it may be on our end and not his. We need to be attuned to his Spirit and tuned in to his frequency. One way to do that is to set the atmosphere. If you want the best quality sound from your TV, you set the audio levels to your liking. If you want to pay attention to a friend or spouse, you get close and make eye contact. If you want to hear God's voice, it's the same.

We need to make sure we're setting the atmosphere for God to talk to us and for us to listen. This is about setting a time and place to hear from him. Setting a time means you are consistent. It should be about the same time every day. And having a set place means you are making it a priority. You set aside a special location just for you and God. Remove all distractions, get locked into God, and then listen. Then go out and put into action what he tells you to do.

keep moving

What are some ways you can set a time and place to hear from God?

attention please

Her sister, Mary, sat at the Lord's feet,
listening to what he taught.
But Martha was distracted.

LUKE 10:39-40 NLT

One day Jesus went to some friends' house for dinner. This was the home of two women whom he knew quite well. One of the women, Martha, had planned out a huge meal. Her sister, Mary, wanted to just spend time with Jesus. Both of those plans were very important. It's great to serve the Lord, but Mary was the one who gave Jesus her full attention. The situation grew tense when Martha asked Jesus to tell Mary to come help her. She was distracted and wanted others to join her.

When we fail to give God our full attention, we miss out on what he has for us. Another way we are distracted is with disobedience. We don't follow through on what he tells us. Our receptiveness to God's voice will only rise to the level of our willingness to be obedient. Don't expect your revelation to exceed your obedience. Don't expect God to talk to you if you're not ready. But do expect him to keep the line open while you follow through and get unstuck.

keep moving

What does it look like for you to give God your full attention?

scary words

The LORD will work out his plans for my life—for your faithful love, O LORD, endures forever. Don't abandon me, for you made me.

PSALM 138:8 NLT

What are the scariest words you've ever heard? I'm not talking about "Boo!" It could be "You're fired." Or maybe "I don't love you anymore." These are the scary words that make us run for cover or stand still, frozen in fear.

The scariest words may be the ones you tell yourself. Looking in the mirror and saying, *I'm not good enough*, is sure to keep you right where you are, stuck in a rut. The thing is that we all feel that way sometimes. Everyone who has ever done something great has had a moment when they didn't feel good enough.

They didn't get past this fear by thinking they were the best. Far from it! They all know what it's like to have a desire to do something great and get excited about seeing it happen. Then comes the crashing blow from the little voice inside that reminds them of their past mistakes and tears down that dream God is building.

Don't listen to it. Instead, drown it out by tuning in to God's Word.

keep moving

Make a list of things the Lord has said about you that make you feel great.

out of the gloom

When that day comes, the deaf will hear the words written in the book. The blind will see out of their gloom and darkness.

ISAIAH 29:18 GW

Do you ever get gloomy? Do you ever feel like nothing is going right? Or maybe you can't shake that little bit of sadness? You want to shake it off, but it feels stuck to you, and it's keeping you stuck. The Lord promises a day when you will be unstuck from that gloom.

The day he's talking about is when God brings salvation to his people. It could mean in the past, when the nation of Israel finally returned from captivity. It could mean that day Jesus spoke of, when he came the first time. It may even refer to a future time, when Jesus finally comes back for all of us. It could even be referring to all three.

Whichever one the Lord is referring to, he is also talking about a present reality you can enjoy. In fact, any time you hear the words written in the Book, the Bible, you can move past your gloom and into the light, ready to go forward in whatever God has planned for you. Don't wait to get rid of your gloom. Turn your ear to God and hear what he has to say.

keep moving

What do you do when you feel gloomy?

haters gonna hate

My enemies say cruel things about me.
They want me to die and be forgotten.

PSALM 41:5 GNT

Yikes! Those are very harsh words. Let's hope that no one ever says that to you or even thinks it. But the truth is that it will likely happen at some point in your life. The best and brightest, the kindest and gentlest always seem to attract enemies. We call those enemies haters. And all they do is hate.

Haters will always demand things from you. They will demand their own way, their own opinion of you, and their own desires over your God-given dreams. On the other hand, real friends don't demand; they dig. They want to know what's inside you because they are just so amazed at what they're seeing come out of you. They will dig deep and find a way to help you live out that dream.

Haters gonna hate, but friends are going to stick. So ignore the haters and get with the real friends, the real encouragers, the real cheerleaders. Find people who speak words of truth and love to you, not deceit and anger.

keep moving

Have you ever been hated on? How did it make you feel?

show them who you are

> You are God's chosen and special people. You are a group of royal priests and a holy nation. God has brought you out of darkness into his marvelous light. Now you must tell all the wonderful things he has done.
>
> 1 Peter 2:9 cev

Do you know who you are? If you do, then show us. If you've put in the work to find out what's driving your heart and you've removed obstacles that have held you back, then let's see it. We want to know because this is what God has designed you to be: uniquely you but incredibly powerful. We can't wait to see what God will do.

If you've spent the energy to work through problems of your circumstances and you've committed to rely consistently on God's rest, then you surely know who you are. It's time to show the haters, the critics, the fence-sitters, and the doubters just who you are. You are God's special person. You are exquisitely designed. You are royal and holy. You are marvelous. You are ready to keep moving forward into God's great future for you. Show it off!

When you understand your identity in Christ, it's like a huge weight has been lifted off your back and a thick curtain has been pulled back from before you. And now it's time to move. Are you ready?

keep moving

What are some ways you can get to the heart of your identity in Christ?

the battlefield

The sinful nature wants to do evil, which is just the opposite of what the Spirit wants. And the Spirit gives us desires that are the opposite of what the sinful nature desires. These two forces are constantly fighting each other, so you are not free to carry out your good intentions.

GALATIANS 5:17 NLT

The battle is real. But it's not right in front of you, visible. It's invisible with a stake in the physical realm. This battle is waged by spiritual forces in physical form though. Within you is your sin nature, which you were born with. The phrase Paul used here, "sinful nature," is literally translated as "flesh," indicating where this nature resides. But its power is from a supernatural source, the domain of evil.

On the other hand are the forces of God. The Holy Spirit resides within you as a believer. And God's Spirit is locked in battle with the ungodly spirits wanting to tear you down. Unfortunately, the battlefield is your very soul.

The battle is real, and it's really important. The reality of your destiny is at stake. When you stay stuck, letting a past hurt or a present habit hold you back, you are unintentionally allowing the Enemy to advance. But when you put those behind you and devote yourself to overcoming the sin nature, you are making progress.

keep moving

Commit today to fighting the battle between sin and the Holy Spirit.

protected

The Lord is faithful, and He will strengthen
and protect you from the evil one.

2 Thessalonians 3:3 nasb

Hearing about spiritual warfare can be unsettling. If there is a battle, then there are winners and losers. And the outcome isn't always assured. What if we lose? What if we give up? What if it's just too much?

The truth is that spiritual warfare is unlike any battle you've ever seen before. You never go into battle with the outcome already written. But that's how it is with spiritual warfare. We already know who will win: us! And we also know how we will win: by the blood of the Lamb.

Another thing we are sure of is that God will protect us. You have nothing to fear from the Evil One. He may attack, he may lie, and he may discourage. But he cannot win. Why? Because God will guard your heart against any attack. He will constantly watch over you. And while you are fighting this battle, you will be able to continue moving forward toward the dream he placed in your heart.

keep moving

When you think about spiritual warfare, what do you think of?

taking captives

We demolish arguments and every pretension that sets itself up against the knowledge of God, and we take captive every thought to make it obedient to Christ.

2 CORINTHIANS 10:5 NIV

In battle, there will be prisoners. The point is not to kill every single combatant. It's to force the other side to surrender. When they do, they are taken prisoner. Now, apply that principle to spiritual warfare. What exactly must be taken captive? Surely not the demonic powers or Satan himself. But there is something that you must surrender and force into submission. Your thoughts.

The battlefield of the mind is a treacherous place. But it's an important one. The Enemy will attack with lies and slander and accusations. But you can dismantle those weapons by searching out any thoughts that are not aligned with God. When you see them, call them out and take them down. Bring them under submission. Remind them of the truth you have in Christ. Apply the beliefs you have from your study of Scripture and your experience with Jesus. And then force them to submit to God rather than wreak havoc in your soul.

keep moving

How might you go about fighting thoughts that are disobedient to God?

not alone

Stand firm against him, and be strong in your faith.
Remember that your family of believers all over the world
is going through the same kind of suffering you are.

1 PETER 5:9 NLT

You are not alone in your fight. It can feel that way sometimes. You encounter an attack, and it feels like nothing else you've ever experienced. You might be tempted to think that no one understands, that no other believer has ever experienced this. But the truth is that every day around the globe God's people are going through what you are going through.

Every single successful Christian believer has gone through tremendous pressure and assault on a spiritual level. The Enemy is not happy when he sees what God's people are doing. He will stop at nothing to keep you from your destiny. His attacks are often relentless. But they are not unique.

Whenever you encounter a spiritual attack, first remind yourself that you are not alone. Take comfort in the fact that, if the Evil One is singling you out, you must be doing something right. Next, pray for those who are undergoing a similar attack. Instead of focusing solely on yourself, turn your attention outward. That will help you get going in the right direction.

keep moving

Remember to pray for others whenever you are under attack.

submit and resist

Submit to God.
Resist the devil,
and he will flee from you.

JAMES 4:7 CSB

Every victory needs a plan. In sports, if you want to win the game, you have to have a game plan. If you're wanting to flip a house, you have to come up with a budget, an investment, and the know-how. If you want to solve a puzzle, how you go about it is as important as how much intellect you bring to the table.

When it comes to spiritual warfare, we need a plan. We have to be aware of the Enemy's schemes, conscious of his mental attacks, and ready to pray. But how? James told us that the game plan is simple, just two words: *submit* and *resist*.

First, any time you feel the Enemy breathing down your neck, submit to God. Make sure you are subject to his authority. Repent of any sins and conform your thoughts to his.

Next, resist the Enemy. Refuse to believe his lies. Counter his deception with the truth. And surround yourself with worship to ensure victory.

keep moving

Make a list of ways you can submit and resist.

no weapon

"No weapon that is formed against you will succeed;
And every tongue that accuses you in judgment you will
condemn."

ISAIAH 54:17 LSB

The attack of the Enemy is real. His weapons are not imaginary. They really do hurt. His lies can cause doubt. His accusations are sharp. His reach is far. But his weapons cannot succeed.

God has promised that no weapon formed against you will succeed. They are still there, and they are being formed, forged in the deep fires of hell. But they are weaker than any weapon God has at his disposal. And the Lord is bringing the full force of his might against the Enemy any time he attacks you.

The weapon formed against us most often is a tongue of accusation. Such accusations don't have to be lies; they can be based in truth. Often it's a way to drag up the past and shove it in your face. The intended result is always to stop you in your tracks. But the outcome will always be defeat for the Enemy if you hold on to God. He has ensured your victory. All you need to do is reach out and take it.

keep moving

What weapon of the Enemy have you ever felt in
your life?

on the prowl

Be on your guard and stay awake.
Your enemy, the devil, is like a roaring lion,
sneaking around to find someone to attack.

1 PETER 5:8 CEV

The Enemy's attack is blatantly obvious to those who study the Word of God. The Enemy is often pictured like a roaring lion. A lion is a fierce beast, the king of the jungle. Lions attack their prey unrelentingly. They are master hunters. Incredibly strong and very agile, they can chase down just about any other animal and kill it.

Here's the thing though. The devil is not a lion. He is *like* a lion. And he can only match the roar of a lion, not its fierceness. The Enemy's plan is to get you scared. If you are scared, you will stop in your tracks. In fact, if you ever find yourself stuck, be on guard because you may be under attack from the Enemy. His roar may be in your ear, but his bite is nothing to be worried about.

Isolation is the key to an attack from the devil. The way a lion hunts is by targeting a lone animal, separating it from the pack, and scaring it into making a poor decision. But if you stay with the pack, then you can overcome the attack. So don't run when you hear the Enemy's roar. Instead, turn to those closest to you.

keep moving

Have you ever experienced the Enemy spiritually roar like a lion?

defeated

On that cross Christ freed himself from the power
of the spiritual rulers and authorities;
he made a public spectacle of them by leading them
as captives in his victory procession.

<small>COLOSSIANS 2:15 GNT</small>

We fight a defeated foe. But what does that mean? Is he not free to roam any longer? No. It means that the end (for him) is assured and the victory (for us) is secured. He is fighting a losing battle, and he knows it. But that actually makes him dangerous. You see, a defeated foe doesn't give up. He is intent on bringing down with him as many as he can.

Whenever we are under attack, the Enemy's goal is not to defeat God. It's to deflate God's people. It's a matter of discouragement and doubt. He wants to make us think that victory is not assured. He wants us to be on the run, away from the front line.

The best way to resist Satan is by doing what he doesn't want us to do. We need to lock arms and keep moving toward God's bright future. Let's come together and remind Satan that he is defeated. Every time we tell others about the cross, it's a reminder to the Enemy that Christ has already defeated him.

keep moving

What does it mean to you that Satan is a defeated foe?

escape plan

No temptation has overtaken you except what is common to mankind. And God is faithful; he will not let you be tempted beyond what you can bear. But when you are tempted, he will also provide a way out so that you can endure it.

1 CORINTHIANS 10:13 NIV

Temptation is a spiritual attack. It is a movement against your soul by the Enemy. We are tempted by our own flesh, being dragged into pleasures and desires from our sin nature. We are also tempted by the world, surrounded by others who are falling into sin. And finally, we can be tempted by the Enemy. One of his weapons is to get us stuck by repeating unhealthy sin behavior.

Whenever you are tempted—by the Enemy, by the world, or by your own flesh—God is aware. And he has made a way out. You are given grace enough to resist any temptation that comes your way. You can stand firm. And you should stand firm.

God wants to see you free and flowing in victory. When you are free from the tangles of sin, you can make up more ground toward your goal. You are able to move around and get moving forward. But sin will only hold you back. How you respond to temptation may be the difference between a dream fulfilled or a dream delayed.

keep moving

What is your escape plan for temptation?

temptation

The Spirit led Jesus into the desert
to be tempted by the devil.

MATTHEW 4:1 GW

When you think of Jesus, one thing that should come to mind is the doctrine of his sinlessness. He was without sin his whole life. His death on the cross represents a perfect sacrifice, a spotless lamb. But that does not mean he could not ever sin. It means that he never did.

At the very beginning of his ministry—in fact, before he even made a public appearance—Jesus was led into a wilderness area. There, he fasted for forty days and nights. He fed himself on the presence of the Father. And then, he faced his greatest trial at that point in his life. The devil himself appeared to tempt him.

When we are tempted, it's part of the natural state of humanity. It's also part of our supernatural state. Since Jesus was tempted, what makes us think we won't be? How he overcame temptation is the most important part of this story. Each time the devil tried to make him fall, Jesus replied with "Scripture says." In other words, he used Scripture against every attack. And we should too! Whenever you feel tempted, simply call on the Word of God to save you.

keep moving

What are some words of the Lord you use
against temptation?

weapons of warfare

*The weapons of our warfare are not of the flesh
but have divine power to destroy strongholds.*

2 CORINTHIANS 10:4 ESV

You are equipped. God has given you powerful weapons, greater than any sword or shield, more powerful than a tank or fighter jet, mightier than a nuclear bomb even. The weapons of warfare that we use are not made by human hands. Instead, they are crafted by divine design.

God knows what you need. And he is aware of the dangers you face. He wants the best for you, so he's selected the best weapons to use. But you need to train in them. Be familiar with the tools he has given you. Spend time in his Word and his presence. Surround your life with worship. That way you are fully trained and prepared.

We never know when an attack is going to come. Sometimes we can feel it coming on, but other times we are taken off guard. That's why it's so important to be fully trained and equipped. If you have the weapons of your warfare with you at all times, you will be ready for any attack. Nothing will get by you because nothing will surprise you. And you won't become stuck in a rut trying to defend yourself.

keep moving

List any spiritual weapons of warfare you have on hand.

armor up

Put on all of God's armor so that you will be able
to stand firm against all strategies of the devil.

EPHESIANS 6:11 NLT

No military power would be successful if they didn't
provide their troops with what they needed to do battle. If
you went to war with limited soldiers, defunct weapons, or
mismatched armor, you would soon find yourself in defeat.
But victory is secure for those who are the best equipped.

God has given you weapons and armor in your
fight against the Enemy. His armor completely surrounds
and protects you. First is the belt of truth, reassuring
you that what you believe is true. Next, the breastplate of
righteousness protects your heart from attack. The shoes
you put on prepare you to share the gospel, and the shield
you take up gives you faith for the journey. Then, put on the
helmet of salvation, reminding yourself that you are saved
and that nothing can stand in your way. Finally, take up the
sword of the Spirit, the Word of God. That way you are fully
armed to attack the Enemy when he roars like a lion.

If you put on the full armor of God daily, by
spending time with him in prayer, you will be ready no
matter what comes your way.

keep moving

Which part of the armor of God do you need the
most help with?

the thief

"The thief comes only to steal and kill and destroy;
I have come that they may have life, and have it to the full."

JOHN 10:10 NIV

Watch out! There's a thief breaking into your home. Well, not a literal thief and not your physical home. But the Enemy wants nothing more than to get inside your heart and tear you apart. He will do anything he can to steal your dream. He would love to kill your motivation. And if he could leave you dead in your tracks, he would be ecstatic. Don't let it happen.

On the other hand, we have a Lord in Jesus, who has come to give us life. It's abundant, overflowing, never-ending, always joyful, and completely loving life. When we focus on him, the thief must leave. He has no place in our hearts as long as Jesus rules there.

So accept Jesus into your heart. Daily give him ownership of your soul. Allow his love to bathe you in light. And give him honor in all you do. That way you won't be stuck robbed by the thief.

keep moving

Have you ever felt robbed by the Enemy?

night and day

The accuser of our brothers and sisters, who accuses them before our God day and night, has been thrown down.

REVELATION 12:10 CSB

What does the Enemy do? Satan has one goal: to take you out. The problem for him is that if you are saved, Christ's blood covers you. The victory he won on the cross is yours in full. So Satan can't keep you from going to heaven. Instead, he will keep you dragged down so you can't do what God wants you to do.

How does he do this? By accusing you. Day and night, night and day, Satan is before the throne of heaven hurling accusations about God's people. He will blame you for everything bad in your life. He will shame you for every mistake you have made. He will condemn you for sin and convince you that you're wrong. That is his only play because he has no other way to take you out.

When you hear something that doesn't sound right—maybe it contradicts what you know to be true about God, or maybe it only leaves you feeling hopeless—then take a look around. Maybe the accuser is trying to convince you of a lie. If that's the case, submit to God and resist the accuser. Let him know that you refuse to believe his lies anymore. And get ready to move on from his accusations.

keep moving

Have you ever felt excessively guilty about something?

greater in you

Dear children, you belong to God. So you have won the victory over these people, because the one who is in you is greater than the one who is in the world.

1 JOHN 4:4 GW

When you start to study the schemes of the Enemy, it can feel a bit heavy. Finding out what he has done, what he can do, and all those who have believed his lies can get you down. But whenever you feel that way, go back to the Word of God. He assures us that no matter how big and bad Satan may seem, the one who is within you is greater still.

If the Enemy is loud, God is louder. If the Enemy roars, God bites his tail. If the Enemy lies, God is truth. If the Enemy accuses, God is love.

God's love is greater. His power is stronger. His Word is mightier. There is nothing we have to fear if the Lord is living inside us. So take courage and continue. There is a dream to fulfill, and God has your back. He is on your side, ready to answer your cry. Let's go!

keep moving

Make a list of reasons you should be glad that God is greater.

can't stop now

"We cannot stop telling about everything
we have seen and heard."

ACTS 4:20 NLT

Many people tried to stop Jesus' movement short. Give
them credit; they did whatever they could do. They jailed
the disciples, beat them, even stoned some of them. But
they just couldn't stop them. Why? Because once Peter
activated the strength God had placed within him, there
was no turning back. This passage is Peter's response to the
demands from the religious leaders who tried to stop him.

When you activate your strengths, knowing that
God is greater in you than the Enemy is in the world, you
just can't stop. Trying to stop what comes next is like trying
to hold your breath. What's inside you just has to come out.
The only way to stop you is to keep you from breathing.

So as long as you have breath in your lungs, keep
activating your strengths. Keep using God's gifts. Keep
leaning on him for protection. Let's find out what God has
put inside us, and let's find ways to get it out of us.

keep moving

What motivates you to keep going?

gate crashers

"I also say to you that you are Peter,
and on this rock I will build my church,
and the gates of Hades will not overpower it."

MATTHEW 16:18 CSB

Gates are really bad offensive weapons. You can't charge while holding a gate. It's very difficult to hurl one at your opponent. The only use for a gate is to let some in while keeping others out. Jesus did not mention the offensive weapons of hell; he only mentioned their defensive ones. That should tell us something. We're to attack!

While there are times we are on defense, keeping our minds clear and our ears from believing the lies of the Enemy, there are also times when we need to attack. Every time you share the gospel, you are on the attack. Every time you share a meal with someone in need, you are on the attack. Every time you use your gifts, you are on the attack. Every time you give to satisfy someone's need, you are on the attack. Every time you decide to move forward in your dream, you are on the attack. These are all ways to keep pushing against the gates of hell.

You may never see these gates fall in your lifetime, but you will see plenty of people escape the clutches of the Enemy and make it safely to God's kingdom. As long as you don't give up!

keep moving

What is one way you can attack the gates of hell today?

november

thankfulness

give thanks

Give thanks to the Lord, for he is good;
his love endures forever.

1 Chronicles 16:34 NIV

What are you thankful for? When you ask yourself that question, often the answer is something that someone did for you. You're thankful to your spouse for making dinner last night. You're thankful to your friends for helping you move. You're thankful for that person who let you merge into traffic. It's the same with God. We are thankful that he saved us, that he strengthens us, that he answers prayer.

But we can also be thankful for who someone is. Thankful that a friend is faithful. Thankful that a spouse is a good listener. Thankful that a boss is caring. And thankful that God is loving.

The Bible tells us in one verse that we can be thankful to God for who he is—a lover who loves forever. His love endures through everything in life. It is unconditional and unrelenting. It is powerful and empowering. No matter what you've done or what you face, his love will always be there. That alone is reason to give him thanks.

keep moving

Make a list of three things you are thankful for today.

devoted

Devote yourselves to prayer.
Be alert and thankful when you pray.

COLOSSIANS 4:2 ISV

For some, staying devoted to praying at a consistent time and place can be difficult. There are plenty of obstacles to keeping that schedule. Your mind wanders. You get tired. You run out of words to say. You're just not sure how to keep going.

One way to make your prayer time stick is to include thankfulness in your devotions. As a part of prayer, thankfulness sets your mind on the things of God. While you recall all that he has done for you, your soul is tuned in to him. You will find that you hear more clearly and that your prayers are more powerful.

Begin and end each time of prayer with thankfulness. Open by thanking God for general things— air in your lungs, sunshine, and family. Then, close by thanking him for more specific things—how he came through for you yesterday, how he answered last week's prayer, and how he will continue meeting your needs. By framing your quiet time with gratitude, you will be setting the stage for an intimate moment with God and launching your day the right way.

keep moving

How can gratitude in prayer help you achieve your goals?

always thankful

I always thank my God for you because of
the grace of God given to you in Christ Jesus.

1 Corinthians 1:4 csb

Do you always have something to thank God about? Sure you do! If you search your memory long enough, you'll find it. If you pay attention during the day, you'll see it. Every day has moments that call for gratitude.

But do you always thank God? Is your life one of continuous gratitude? Most likely you go through phases during the day when you're grumpy or angry. That's normal. But even in the down times, we can be thankful. The Scriptures tell us to be always thankful. Not just to look out for things to be thankful for but also to be thankful for the things we don't realize call for gratitude.

When you are blessed, give thanks. That's easy. But when you run into a problem, thank God for giving you the endurance to meet the challenge. When someone hurts you, give God thanks for empowering you to forgive. When you are bored, give God thanks for passion in life. In whatever you do, there is a moment when thankfulness is the right response.

keep moving

Today, thank God in the most difficult moment of
your day.

bless you

You will be blessed in every way, and you will be able to keep on being generous. Then many people will thank God when we deliver your gift.

2 CORINTHIANS 9:11 CEV

Thanksgiving produces thanksgiving. Just like blessing brings blessings. When you bless others, God will bless you in return. And then you can be even more giving. It's a divine cycle that the Lord loves to see in your life.

In the same way, thanksgiving can turn into more thanksgiving. It's a lot like when you say, "Thank you," to someone and they say, "No, thank *you*." Thanksgiving is contagious. When you are thankful, others want to be thankful along with you. And when you see someone being thankful, your mind goes into gratitude mode.

Another way that thanksgiving produces more thanksgiving is in how we respond. When we are thankful, we want to find more ways to be thankful. We want to look out for or do things that will produce that thankfulness. And then God will respond with more blessing and more opportunity. Gratitude creates generosity. And generosity creates gratitude.

keep moving

List some ways that you can multiply gratitude.

message received

Since everything God created is good,
we should not reject any of it but receive it with thanks.

1 TIMOTHY 4:4 NLT

Every good gift is from God (see James 1:17). If it's good, it's God. And if it's good, we should be thankful for it. When we are thankful for what God gives us, that gift cannot be corrupted. It becomes sanctified to our life.

Here's how this works. When you are ungrateful for a gift, you shift into entitlement mode. You feel like you deserve more than what you are given. The focus is on you. But when you are grateful, the focus shifts from the gift to the giver. Now, you recognize the Lord as the author of your life and the giver of your gifts. You see each gift as it's meant to be. And you are less likely to misuse it.

Everything in your life can be created by God for good. The key is to be thankful, to be grateful for what he has given you. When you do that, you can use anything that comes your way as a means to keep moving in life. Nothing can stop grateful people from seeing the dream God placed in their heart come true.

keep moving

Make a list of gifts you've received from God this week and thank him for them.

answer to anxiety

Do not be anxious about anything, but in every situation, by prayer and petition, with thanksgiving, present your requests to God.

PHILIPPIANS 4:6 NIV

The world is more anxious than ever. Worry is at the top of everyone's to-do list. Mental health is at an all-time low, thanks, in no small part, to the weight of stress we all bear. How do we get out of this hole?

The answer to your anxiety is thanksgiving. Studies show that an attitude of gratitude can lower blood pressure, increase good chemicals in your brain, reduce the risk of heart disease, and improve your outlook on life. All these factors contribute to clearing out the anxiety that may be holding you back in life.

Another way that thanksgiving is the answer to your anxiety is a spiritual application. When you are grateful, your soul searches for the good things in life. When you commit to being thankful, you are sending your spirit on a scavenger hunt. You are trying to look at every single thing in your life from a positive point of view. Instead of always expecting the worst, you are anticipating the best. And God's Holy Spirit will encounter your spirit in the middle of your thanksgiving.

keep moving

How can you better hunt down gratitude in your life?

strength and shield

The LORD is my strength and my shield;
in him my heart trusts, and I am helped;
my heart exults, and with my song I give thanks to him.

PSALM 28:7 ESV

Grateful people rarely get stuck in life. They hardly find time to ponder the negatives. They are moving forward in life toward God's plan because they are constantly reassured of his goodness and mercies, of his overwhelming gifts for them.

Gratitude is like a protective armor. It guards your heart against bitterness by constantly infusing you with positivity. It acts as a barrier against negative self-talk. It creates a shield that wards off the evil schemes of the Enemy. When you are grateful, you are protected from spiritual attack because you just know that any attack will ultimately fail.

Put this strength and shield to use. Whenever someone says something negative to you, raise up that shield of gratitude. Whenever something bad happens, pull on the strength of thankfulness. Find the positive in any situation. If you happen to encounter a struggle, thank God for the opportunity. That very act will be all you need to keep going forward in life.

keep moving

How has gratitude strengthened you in the past?

overflowing

All this is for your benefit, so that the grace that is reaching more and more people may cause thanksgiving to overflow to the glory of God.

2 CORINTHIANS 4:15 NIV

Do you want a little joy or a lot of joy? Well, how much gratitude you have may be the determining factor. These two are locked together in your life. When you are more grateful, you are more joyous. When you are looking for reasons to rejoice, you are more grateful. They go hand in hand. And the best part is, when one overflows, the other one is sure to do the same.

Your joy can also cause other people's thankfulness to overflow. When you have a good and pleasing attitude, people want to be close to you. They want to know what's so great. They are curious about your attitude. They will start to see more positive things in their life and have reason to be grateful. And when you are overflowing in gratitude, they will see it and rejoice along with you.

Gratitude can be a fuel to your dreams coming true. As you are more and more thankful in life, others will rejoice. As their joy overflows, your gratitude increases beyond measure. Soon, you will be sprinting into God's best for your life.

keep moving

How can you make someone rejoice today by your attitude of gratitude?

what rules your heart

Let the peace that comes from Christ rule in your hearts.
For as members of one body you are called to live in peace.
And always be thankful.

COLOSSIANS 3:15 NLT

You have control of your own heart. You get to decide who or what will rule it. Whoever or whatever rules your heart will call the shots in your life. Making decisions and choosing values are what your heart does.

What rules your heart? Is it negativity and doubt? Are you ruled by sin and shame? Maybe it's regret and anxiety. How about making a shift? You can change today. When peace rules your heart, you can make every decision in confidence. You are relaxed and ready to move forward. You are fully equipped to handle any storm. You are prepared for the struggle ahead. Why? Because the supernatural peace of God will provide clarity and assurance in every decision.

Peace can rule your heart. And the Bible tells us how. The way to put peace in control of your heart is through thankfulness. As you are grateful for your life, the peace of God washes over you. It's like a cleansing rain that comes at just the right time. It's like a morning ray of sunshine, breaking into every area of your life. It's the way to take hold of the reins of your life and start moving forward.

keep moving
Make a list of things you need peace about.

victory

Thank God that he gives us the victory
through our Lord Jesus Christ.

1 CORINTHIANS 15:57 GW

What are you facing today? Did you know you already have victory over it? The battle is won, the outcome secure. You just need to accept it. You're going to win. The victory for your very soul was won on the cross. When Jesus died for you, he freed you from your past, from your pain, and from your passions. That victory is within reach. All you have to do is reach out and take it. And we thank God every day for it.

The victory over your present problem has also been won. It's secured, and it's within reach. Why not start thanking God right now? You can start every day either worrying about the problems or thanking God for the solutions. You can look at your schedule and be filled with anxiety or gratitude. You can look at the bright side or the dark side. It's up to you.

Pray each day, *God, thank you for winning the battle. It's already won. The victory is already mine. I can't wait to see how it will work out, but I know it will. Thank you.*

keep moving

What victory do you need today? Start thanking
God now.

let me tell you

I will praise you, LORD, with all my heart
and tell about the wonders you have worked.

PSALM 9:1 CEV

Have you ever kept a secret? It's hard. You learn something so fascinating that you want to share it. You can't keep it in. Guess what? It's no secret what God has done for you, so you can spill the beans. Let everyone know.

Thanks is something we do with our mouth. Sure, you can live in such a way that all your actions are in response to your gratitude. Generosity is a direct result of an attitude of gratitude. Joy and happiness are emotions that accompany it. But expressing thanksgiving verbally gives us and others clarity about the gratitude we feel inside.

Don't just make a list of what you are thankful for. Start reading it out loud. Say it to yourself, first of all. Look in the mirror and say, "I'm so thankful for what God has done for you!" Talking to yourself in a positive way is such a great start to your day.

Next, start telling others. Don't wait either. Every time something good happens, return that thanks right away. Say it out loud, in front of others. Thank God in the midst of his people. Tell of his great wonders. And soon you'll find others doing the same thing.

keep moving

Make a point to make your thankfulness known today.

for all people

I ask you to pray for everyone.
Ask God to help and bless them all,
and tell God how thankful you are for each of them.

1 TIMOTHY 2:1 CEV

Whom are you thankful for? I'm sure you're thankful for a good mom and dad, a caring grandparent, a coach or teacher who invested in you, or a boss who looked out for you. It's easy to feel thankful for these people, but do we express it? You can thank God for them, and you can also thank them directly. Set aside time to write a note, send a text, or make a phone call to let them know just how thankful you are for them.

But that's only one group of people. What about the rest? The Bible says we should be thankful for everyone we come in contact with. The grumpy cashier at the grocery store. The person who raced by us in their car, honking impatiently. The one who was critical of us. The neighbor who never waves. We can be thankful for them. As long as they're alive, they have an opportunity to change their attitude. But for you, be thankful that you get to encounter them. As iron sharpens iron, they can help you with your patience and endurance, and you can show them how good it is to change their life.

keep moving

Make a list of those people you are thankful for and write a note to at least one of them.

everything always

Always thank God the Father for everything
in the name of our Lord Jesus Christ.

EPHESIANS 5:20 GW

Start writing out your thanksgiving list. Not what you'll eat but what you'll be thankful for. Start now because you don't want to be caught off guard, not knowing what to say when your turn comes at the dinner table. But here's a little trick that you can use to help you get started: everything always. Be thankful about everything. Be thankful always.

If you start writing that list now, you won't finish it by the time the turkey is on the table. Why? Because there is something to be thankful for in everything that happens to you. Everything you go through has a purpose in God's divine design, so be thankful. Everything that others say to you can help shape you into the Christlike person God wants you to be, so be thankful. Everything that tries to get in your way is an opportunity to show off God's power, so be thankful.

And be thankful always. Practice that attitude of gratitude. Use it like a muscle, getting stronger every day. Start now, and by the time Thanksgiving rolls around, you can leave your list at home. You'll have it memorized.

keep moving

Practice making a list of gratitude today.

thanks for growing

We ought always to give thanks to God for you, brothers,
as is right, because your faith is growing abundantly, and
the love of every one of you for one another is increasing.

2 THESSALONIANS 1:3 ESV

Can you see it growing in other people's lives? Their faith.
Their love. Their devotion to God. Are you close enough
to get a sense of it? Are you paying attention at the right
times? Let's hope so. Because it's happening, and it's giving
you an invitation to say thanks.

Be thankful to God for things happening in the lives
of others, not just your own life. Spend some time thinking
about how your friend or family member got good news
today. Maybe they've been struggling with an issue and
received a breakthrough. Perhaps they were always down,
and now their attitude is turning around.

When you thank God for other people, you will
begin to see growth in new areas. Focusing on your own
issues is certainly a way to grow in those areas. But when
you turn your attention outward, you start to flex your
spiritual muscles. It's like when you start a new workout
and you learn that there are other muscle groups you didn't
know you had. The best way to grow is to start thanking
God for the growth you see in others.

keep moving

Take a moment to think of one friend and give God
thanks for their growth.

more joy

You have given me greater joy than those who have
abundant harvests of grain and new wine.

PSALM 4:7 NLT

God has so much in store for you. He wants to fill you with
greater joy. That means that everything he has planned for
you is for your benefit. It will be like a party just waiting to
happen. It's better than abundant harvests. It will make you
happier than any wine. It's ready to start today!

God wants to see you happy. And there's nothing
wrong with that. Whatever happened to happiness? In our
search for holiness, we've redefined happiness. Joy, for us,
is an attitude that is disconnected from our circumstances.
We are joyful even if bad stuff happens to us. But happiness
is contingent only on good things happening to us. But
what's wrong with that? God wants good things to happen
to you. He is ready to make that happen and to make you
happy. And that happiness will fuel you to the next phase
of life.

keep moving

What is one good thing that happened to you
recently that made you happy?

futile minds

Although they knew God, they did not glorify him as God or give him thanks, but they became futile in their thoughts and their senseless hearts were darkened.

ROMANS 1:21 NET

It's futile to think any other way than the way that brings gratitude to your soul. When you refuse to thank God, though, your thinking becomes destructive. Your brain begins to short-circuit on negativity, and your way of thinking is completely clouded. Lift that cloud with an attitude of gratitude.

You know someone who refuses to be happy. The best things in life come their way, and they find some reason to be sad or disappointed about it. The root cause is a lack of thanksgiving.

Gratitude transforms your thought life. You go from futile to fulfilled, from a dead end to alive again. Our brains are programed to do exactly what we want them to do. If you want to see the negativity behind every event, your brain will do that for you. If you want to see sunshine, your brain will help you peek over every cloud in life. It's up to you though. And it begins with thanksgiving. If you feel stuck in a cycle of negativity, try pulling yourself out with some gratitude.

keep moving

When have you experienced negative thoughts that don't seem to go away?

a sacrifice

Through Him then, let's continually offer up a sacrifice of praise to God, that is, the fruit of lips praising His name.

HEBREWS 13:15 NASB

A sacrifice is something we do that we don't want to do. We might do it grudgingly, wishing we were somewhere else, but we do it because it needs to be done. That's why people have those bumper stickers that say, "I'd rather be fishing." Sure, they'd rather be somewhere else. But they know the power of being where they're supposed to be and doing what they're supposed to do.

A sacrifice means you go against your overwhelming feeling. A lot of times we encounter troubles and want to throw our hands up. We feel like griping and complaining. We feel like letting someone have it. But that's not what we do. Instead, we offer up a sacrifice of praise. "I'm going to praise you anyway, Lord." And then we offer up a sacrifice of thanksgiving. "I'm not sure what you'll do with this situation, God, but thank you for bringing it into my life. Now I have a front-row seat to your awesome power."

A sacrifice is never a bad thing. It means taking what you want and laying it down for what you need. We all need an attitude of gratitude. Without it, we are stuck in neutral going nowhere. With it, we are destined for great things.

keep moving

What kind of sacrifice of praise can you give today?

God will add

"From them will come songs of thanksgiving and the sound of rejoicing. I will add to their numbers, and they will not be decreased."

JEREMIAH 30:19 NIV

Do you like math? You either love it or hate it, probably. For most of us, we're glad to have a calculator on our phone now. We're happy to have algebra and geometry behind us. Let the experts handle the math. We've got other things to worry about.

God loves math. He loves to multiply your blessings. He loves to subtract your problems. He loves to divide the Enemy's schemes, driving them in seven different directions. And he loves to add to your life. He will add to your number of days. He will add more and more joy. He will add blessing on blessing and grace for grace. He will add to your life when you are thankful to him.

The thanksgiving of our life is one half of a divine math equation. God works out all the details, putting your life into proper context and moving behind the scenes. Our end of the equation is to thank him. We sit back and watch him work the math and then respond in gratitude. He has figured out the best for your life, and he can't wait to see it play out. And we need to thank him for it.

keep moving

What is lacking in your life that you need God to add to?

get in there

Enter his gates with thanksgiving and his courts with praise.
Give thanks to him and bless his name.

PSALM 100:4 CSB

Why do we go to church? Why do we enter into times of praise and worship? Why do we gather together with other believers? Why is that part of our spiritual growth? Part of the reason is that church services are times to share in gratitude.

An attitude of gratitude grows when we gather. If you come together with someone else who shares what God has done, your gratitude grows. When you hear a testimony of his divine intervention, of his amazing love, of his saving grace, you can't help but respond. You can't wait to share your own testimony too.

When you enter God's presence with others, be ready to share. Get ready to be a part of the praise. He wants to use your life, your words of victory and vision, to lift others up, to motivate them, to get them unstuck. And you will hardly ever be stuck if you are the one leading the procession. So get in there and start thanking God.

keep moving

What word of thanksgiving will you bring next time you gather with others?

make it known

You will say in that day: "Give thanks to the LORD, call upon his name, make known his deeds among the peoples, proclaim that his name is exalted."

ISAIAH 12:4 ESV

What are you known for? Whatever it is, others can see it in you. They take one look at you, have one conversation with you, or share one cup of coffee with you, and they know who you are.

What if others knew us as thankful people? What if someone said about them, "Well, I'm not sure what their job is, but they are always so grateful." We can make ourselves known as people who are always living out gratitude. Just think how that can change our lives. Just think how people will respond to us. Just imagine how our lives can impact others.

Part of the dream God has placed in your life is to be a leader. Maybe you're not a business manager, an entrepreneur, or a CEO, but you can be a spiritual leader, helping others see the power of gratitude. You can be a motivational leader, sharing your story of how God is leading you. So make your gratitude known today and lead others into thankfulness.

keep moving

I challenge you to call two people and express thankfulness to them today.

what a wonderful sound

"The sounds of joy and laughter. The joyful voices of bridegrooms and brides will be heard again, along with the joyous songs of people bringing thanksgiving offerings to the Lord."

JEREMIAH 33:11 NLT

What sound do you just love to hear? If you're a grandparent, it might be the sound of laughter from your grandchild. If you're a sports fan, it's the sound of the crowd cheering on your team. If you're a gearhead, it's probably the sound of an engine purring or the roar of a race car.

For all of us, there is one sound that should get us going: the sound of joy. Whenever something good happens in our lives, we should speak up about it. We need to be ready with thanksgiving. It's not just a once-a-year thing. It's a continual cause for celebration.

When you make thanksgiving a part of your vocabulary, you will be a wonderful sound to those around you. You will attract the right kind of attention from others. They will want to be near you as you talk about what God has done. You will be the source of such a wonderful sound.

And as you make that sound of thanksgiving, you will be fueling your soul as well. You will be repeating the words that set you on fire for God.

keep moving

How do you like to proclaim thanksgiving for what God has done?

good is on its way

Good will come to the one who lends generously
and conducts his business fairly.

PSALM 112:5 CSB

The outcome of gratitude is generosity. When you give
thanks, you also want to give something to show for it. You
want to put a gift behind the gift you received. It's better to
give than to receive, and giving sparks even more gratitude.

An attitude of gratitude will shrivel up and die if it
encounters a stingy mindset. To grab on to what you have
and hoard it will only lead to negative self-talk. It will make
you think that you have less than you need. But when you
are generous, you see how God has blessed you. All you
want to do is thank him for it. And good is on its way too.

God has planned a special blessing for those who are
generous with what he's given them. When you are willing
to open your hand to give to others, God is able to fill
your hand with what you need. Why not try it today? Go
ahead and see if he won't send good your way when you are
generous with what you have and grateful for what he gives.

keep moving

What is one "good" that you need to come to
you today?

gains

One person gives freely, yet gains even more;
another withholds unduly, but comes to poverty.

PROVERBS 11:24 NIV

Giving does not leave you with less. It opens you up for more. It's not taking anything away from you. It's using what you have to show the world how great God is. Giving is the physical way we show gratitude. And it will also help us. Every act of generosity gains more than it gives away. But every act of stinginess loses more than it has tried to save.

Your attitude determines the direction of your life. It can also affect the velocity of your dreams. If you have the right attitude, you will be headed in the right direction. An attitude of gratitude puts you on the same path of God. And an act of generosity will increase your momentum. You will start to see yourself meeting more and more goals. You will get closer and closer to your dream sooner than you can imagine. That's what is in store for you as you give freely from what God has freely given you.

keep moving

What is one way you can give freely today?

he is good

Give thanks to the LORD, because he is good;
his love is eternal.

PSALM 136:1 GNT

There are so many reasons to thank God. We thank him for our life and salvation. We thank him for his provision and protection. We thank him for what he's done for our friends and family. We thank him for our church, our country, our world. We thank him for a relaxing afternoon and good rains for the land. We thank him for the strength to go just one more day.

But even if he never did any of those, there is one reason to give thanks. He is good. His goodness is reason to rejoice. His goodness is the basis of our thanksgiving. His goodness is why we are grateful.

We could serve another god, but there is no other god as good as our God. We could choose to serve money, but the love of money is the root of all evil. We could choose to serve our country, but every nation of the world will one day bow to him. So why not serve and love and thank the God of heaven, who is good beyond measure. He is so good he will pour his goodness out on you. He will keep you moving forward, never looking back, if you thank him for his goodness.

keep moving

What is one characteristic of God's goodness that gets you excited?

i can't stop

I never stop thanking God for you.
I always remember you in my prayers.

Ephesians 1:16 GW

There is no reason to stop thanking God. His goodness has no limit. His power has no end. His blessing has no off switch. He is good, day and night, night and day. So we always have a reason to thank God. We just can't stop.

If you ever feel stuck in life, maybe it's because you stopped thanking him. You got off track on some other concern. You got distracted by some negative thought. You took your eyes off God and put them on your own problem. And now, you've found yourself stopped and stuck for not thanking him.

The first step is recognizing it happened. Seeing that you've stopped thanking him, you found the problem. The second step is an easy one: just start thanking him. Find something right where you are to thank him for. Then add another thanks. Keep adding thanks until you feel the momentum in your life.

As you commit to thanking God in every way so you just can't stop, you will find traction in life. You begin to see obstacles differently and start to hear discouragement with a different tune. Now you are ready to move forward in life, committed to seeing this dream fulfilled.

keep moving

If you've stopped thanking God, how will you start again?

how to be blessed

A generous person will be blessed,
for he shares his food with the poor.

PROVERBS 22:9 CSB

Do you have more of something than you need? If you have more clothing than you can wear, a fridge with more food than you can eat, a bank account with more money than you can spend, that's an indication to give. Generosity is when we share with others. It doesn't have to be financial. It can be sharing of our time. It can be sharing our presence or our advice. It doesn't matter what you share. The act of sharing is what causes your blessing.

A generous person is one who responds well with gratitude. A generous person sees someone in need and immediately asks, "How can I help?" That's because they've been helped. They are grateful for that help and want to share it. And now they have enough to help others too.

One thing to be grateful for is the surplus you have. In some area of your life, you have more than enough. And that means you can share that with others. You express your gratitude by your generosity to others.

keep moving

What do you have that you can bless someone
with today?

what God is due

I will give thanks to the LORD because of his righteousness; I will sing the praises of the name of the LORD Most High.

PSALM 7:17 NIV

God is worthy of your praise. Not just because he created you and saved you. Not just because he gave you great gifts, physical and spiritual. Not just because he answered your prayers. But because of how he is: righteous.

The righteousness of God is the reason you are here today. Without his righteousness bestowed on us, we would be left trying to make our own lives complete and perfect. We would be struggling to live a holy life all alone. We would be wandering in the dark trying to find a way.

God's righteousness is greater than any of our sins. It's stronger than any habit you have. It's more powerful than anything in your past and mightier than anything in your future. It is what defines his love for you. It's what declares his grace over you.

Giving thanks for his righteousness means you acknowledge that he alone can save you. And you are declaring that he alone is holy. You have given up trying on your own. Now, you lean into him to provide all you need and keep you moving forward toward the dream he placed in your heart.

keep moving

How do you think being grateful for God's righteousness keeps you unstuck in life?

freely give

"Heal the sick, raise the dead, cure those with leprosy,
and cast out demons. Give as freely as you have received!"

MATTHEW 10:8 NLT

What did you pay to get saved? Nothing. It was free. Your
salvation, your breakthrough, your sanctification, your
wisdom and grace and empowerment. It was all free. That
means someone gave it to you and you didn't do anything
for it. God is the One. And now, we are called to give like
we received, with no strings attached.

Find something in your life that was a gift from
God. Perhaps it was some moment when you needed him
most, a pain that you needed healed, or a lacking that you
needed filled. Now look for that in someone else. Do you
know someone who is feeling down? Depressed? Anxious?
Worried about what comes next? Disappointed about what
just happened? Needing a pick-me-up or a "save me"?

Then jump into action. You're ready! God has
already equipped you when he rescued you from the same
situation. He freely gave you a hand, and now you can
share that with others. It's part of the reason he gave you
that dream in the first place. It's just one facet of his will for
your life. Let your attitude of gratitude for what you've been
given be the reason you share with others.

keep moving

What is something God has given you that you can
share with others?

donating life

We know what love is because Jesus gave his life for us.
This is why we must give our lives for each other.

1 JOHN 3:16 CEV

The most famous verse in the Bible is John 3:16. Many know it by heart. "For God so loved the world that he gave his one and only son" (NIV). That one single passage has the entire gospel message wrapped up in it. Those simple words have meant life to billions of souls for thousands of years.

But what about another 3:16? The first letter of John—not to be confused with the gospel of John—shares so much about God's love for us. Word by word, it's full of reasons to be thankful. And at the heart is 1 John 3:16. In an echo of what John 3:16 says, we hear that Jesus gave up his life for us. But now, we are to jump into action. Gratitude drives us to do the same. To be like Christ means we act like him. We give, or donate, our lives just as he did.

When you donate your life, you are not giving up on your dreams. In fact, it's the fulfillment of that dream. It's the way you keep moving. Giving will propel you to the next level because you will be living out the very will of God for your life, being like Jesus.

keep moving

What is one way you can donate your life today?

december

the gift of Jesus

a gift from God

Thanks be to God for his indescribable gift!

2 CORINTHIANS 9:15 NIV

What do you want for Christmas this year? When we were kids, we would sit and write out a Christmas list. We spent hours poring over catalogs, trying to decide on the perfect toys. If we put too many on the list, we might not get anything. So we had to be strategic.

As adults, it's a little less of a problem. Sometimes it's hard to think of anything we want. If we have kids, Christmas is usually all about them and less about what we're getting. You might even be "hard to shop for," but that just means you know the power that giving has over receiving.

With God, we don't have to be shy though. He is ready and willing to give us gifts. He loves to give to his children year-round. But Christmas does represent the height of his giving. What he gave us in Jesus Christ was so amazing that it's difficult to put into words. He offered it to us before we could even make a list. Why is this gift so indescribable? Part of that is because through the one gift of Jesus Christ, we have so many more gifts. We have new life. We have freedom. There's no reason to be stuck in life when you have the indescribable gift of God.

keep moving

What is your favorite Christmas gift—one you got and one you gave?

hope

Let your hope make you glad.
Be patient in time of trouble and never stop praying.

ROMANS 12:12 CEV

Of all the gifts from God, hope may be the most essential in this world. It's the gift that keeps on giving. Hope is the belief that tomorrow will be a better day. It's the feeling that things will turn out. And it's not based on emotion, but it's based on a promise. God has told us time and time again that he will come through, he will do it for us, he will come and rescue us. So let's put our hope in him.

Think back to the last year. You've had ups and downs. You've had good times and bad. It's easy to remember the troubles you've had. The fond memories are a little fuzzier, maybe. You might need some time to think of the blessings you've received. But through it all, you've made it. You endured. You were patient in those times of trouble. Why? Because you never stopped. You never gave up. On the other side of trouble was even more hope. The fact that you endured the trouble meant the next trouble somehow felt lighter.

keep moving

Think of a time this year that you endured trouble because of your hope.

peace

By faith we have been made acceptable to God. And now, thanks to our Lord Jesus Christ, we have peace with God.

ROMANS 5:1 CEV

Are you looking forward to a peaceful holiday? You're probably not entirely sure it will be restful. You might have family coming into town, a party to host, gifts to buy and wrap. The list goes on and on, and it's sure to rob you of peace. Wouldn't it be nice to know that God has a gift of peace just waiting for you?

God gives us peace through the gift of his Son. He begins by making peace with us. We are no longer enemies of God; we are his friends. He loves us and cares for us, and he made the move to bring peace among us. And because of that peace, we can have peace with others. God is working behind the scenes right now to resolve conflict and make your relationships better, tying you in a strong bond with others and empowering you to forgive each other, wiping the slate clean. But it all starts with that peace we have with God. That peace will keep you unstuck and moving forward in life. Accept it today.

keep moving

Describe what a peaceful holiday season looks like to you.

joy to come

"Now you are having pain. But I'll see you again,
and your hearts will rejoice, and no one will
take your joy away from you."

JOHN 16:22 ISV

The holiday season is not always full of joy for everyone. It can be a reminder of loss. Maybe you've lost a job this year. You could have lost a home or a car. Perhaps a friend or family member passed away suddenly or just is no longer in your life. Gathering around the Christmas tree this year will definitely be different.

Although you're in pain now, there is joy to come. It's hard to see or even feel that joy right now. But it's there, and no one can take it from you. The joy that God gives is unreturnable. It's nontransferable. It's joy everlasting.

Joy is not just a grin-and-bear-it emotion. It's not about enduring pain and trying to have a good attitude about it. It's real gladness. It's happiness over what God is doing in your life. So ask God to show you where he is showing up, and then be glad about what he is doing there. Ask him to replace your sorrow with joy, to take away your pain and place happiness within once again. That way, you have even more reason to keep going in life.

keep moving

What is one thing you are sad about today and one thing you are happy about today?

love is the center

Faith, hope, and love abide, these three;
but the greatest of these is love.

1 Corinthians 13:13 esv

What's love got to do with it? What role does love play in the Christmas story? Plenty! Love is not just a gift that God gives us through Jesus Christ. It's the motivating factor for all his gifts. The Bible tells us that God gave us his Son, Jesus Christ, because he loves us. At the center of every gift he gives is love.

That's why love is the greatest of any other gift he gives. Hope and faith are powerful. Peace is amazing. Joy is overflowing in the life of the believer. But love fills all of us to the brim. There is nothing in life that more love cannot improve. Every aspect of your life needs the love of God looking out for it.

When you apply the gift of God's love to your life, you are bound for more. You will be motivated to work harder and go further. You won't be held back by burdens and struggles. You will be unstoppable in this life. So accept freely God's greatest gift today.

keep moving

How can a deeper understanding of God's love help you this season?

it was fulfilled

All this took place to fulfill what was spoken
by the Lord through the prophet.

MATTHEW 1:22 CSB

The story of Jesus has been told over and over again for centuries. In fact, it may be the most told story of all time. But did you know that the story was told even before it happened? The Old Testament is full of prophecies about the future. One aspect that came to be a repeated theme was the coming of a Messiah. The fulfillment of those prophecies happened and has become part of recorded history.

God is so concerned with your life that, thousands of years ago, he led people to write about the Messiah. He gave a recorded message to let them know something great was on its way. He wanted everyone to have a heads-up. God was going to do it.

In your own life, God is letting you know that something good is just ahead. Don't give up. Don't stop now. You're so close to achieving what you've always dreamed about. Why should you not believe the one whose prophecies have come true time and time again?

keep moving

How does it make you feel knowing that God's
prophecies have come true?

God is with us

"She will give birth to a son and will call him Immanuel (which means 'God is with us')."

ISAIAH 7:14 NLT

Do you have a nickname? Something that only those closest to you call you. It's based not on your given name but probably on some characteristic that is so *you*. Maybe it's an inside joke about something that you did long ago. Whatever it is, it's special to those around you.

Jesus has some nicknames. He is known as the Messiah, Christ. He is the Alpha and Omega. In the Old Testament, he has many, many nicknames. Perhaps the greatest of those is Immanuel. The name literally means "God is with us." And it reveals so much about who Jesus is.

There is no other religion on earth that tells of a god who is interested in human affairs enough to visit them in the flesh. But our God did. He looked down and saw our helpless state and decided to intervene. He showed up as a vulnerable baby, needing the strength of the Father. He lived his life as an ordinary man. He died as any other human would. But then he was resurrected as we all will be one day. His life fully encompassed every experience we have had, will have, or could have. And that makes all the difference in the world.

keep moving

What is one thing you're going through that Jesus did as well?

o little town

Bethlehem Ephrath, you are one of the smallest towns in the nation of Judah. But the LORD will choose one of your people to rule the nation—someone whose family goes back to ancient times.

MICAH 5:2 CEV

God loves to use the small things in life. He chose a small nation, Israel, to represent his salvation to all people. He chose David, the smallest of all his brothers, to be the greatest king in Israel's history. He chose a wee little man, Zacchaeus, to share a big story of God's grace. And in the Christmas story, he chose a small town called Bethlehem as the stage of the biggest moment in human history.

God could have chosen any place he wished to bring Jesus into the world. Jerusalem, with its temple and religious order, he did not choose. Rome, the center of the global empire at the time, he overlooked. But Bethlehem was the place that God gave prominence.

Think about your own life. If you feel small, that's a good thing. God loves to make something big of things that are small. If you feel overlooked or skipped, God has not forgotten you. Looking back over the last year, you may see times when you felt out of place or underappreciated. God still has his eye on you and wants to do something big through you.

keep moving

What is your biggest unfulfilled dream or goal?

anointed

The Spirit of the Sovereign Lord is on me, because the Lord has anointed me to proclaim good news to the poor. He has sent me to bind up the brokenhearted, to proclaim freedom for the captives and release from darkness for the prisoners.

Isaiah 61:1 NIV

Jesus came with purpose in life. That was most evident when he was baptized and commissioned. As Jesus came up out of the water, the Holy Spirit descended on him as a dove. And the Father declared for all to hear, "This is my Son, whom I love; with him I am well pleased" (Matthew 3:17 NIV). Afterward, Jesus entered a synagogue in his hometown and read the words above from the scroll of Isaiah. He announced that the words of the prophet were being fulfilled in his own life and ministry.

What Jesus did for us in his public ministry was beyond compare. He provided good news for us while we were poor in spirit. In all ways, we never have enough, but when we admit our shortcomings, he fills in the gaps. He also releases us from captivity, clearing our sight. He mends our broken hearts and gives us a new spirit. Nothing can stop us. And it's all because of what he has done for us.

keep moving

How have you seen these different aspects of Jesus' ministry in your own life?

bringing justice

The LORD says, "Here is my servant, whom I strengthen—the one I have chosen, with whom I am pleased. I have filled him with my Spirit, and he will bring justice to every nation."

ISAIAH 42:1 GNT

Jesus knew who he was and what he was called to do. The Father had told him, and the Holy Spirit had anointed him. He was ready to see it happen too. And he was determined to fulfill his calling. That calling meant that he needed to be razor focused on his ministry.

At the heart of the fulfillment of Jesus' ministry is justice. You might think of justice as getting what you deserve. It's God playing fair, right? Not exactly. We don't get what we deserve because, after all, we all deserve a death sentence for our sin. Through grace, we get what we don't deserve. Justice means we are made right again. It entails God reshaping us into something that can overcome every obstacle in life. It involves him placing his Holy Spirit on your life and showing you the way to live right. In fact, the best way you can respond to God's justice is to live a life worthy of your calling, chasing every dream and fulfilling every promise God has given you. He has equipped you to run. So let's do it.

keep moving

What is one unfulfilled promise you still want to see fulfilled this year?

all nations

"I saw a human form, a son of man, arriving in a whirl of clouds. He came to The Old One and was presented to him. He was given power to rule—all the glory of royalty. Everyone—race, color, and creed—had to serve him. His rule would be forever, never ending. His kingly rule would never be replaced."

DANIEL 7:13-14 MSG

Daniel had this vision of Jesus Christ. He saw someone who looked like the Son of Man, a biblical phrase that indicates the Messiah. And when this Son of Man comes, he comes in power and glory. He makes a statement upon entry. And he also makes a statement by whom he invites to join him.

Everyone's invited. There are no restrictions on who can come to join Jesus in the kingdom. There is no bouncer at the door keeping you from entering. Every race. Every color. Every creed can come on in. Jesus blesses all nations of the world.

No matter what you've been through or what you've done, Jesus invites you in. You can join him in his mission to the world. You can be part of the blessing, being blessed and blessing others. No wonder he has such a great plan for your life! Don't stay stuck but get going today.

keep moving

Who is someone you think would never respond to an invitation from Jesus? Pray that they receive him this Christmas season.

highly favored

The angel came to her and said, "Greetings,
you who are highly favored! The Lord is with you!"

LUKE 1:28 ISV

What was God looking for? When he chose to send his Son
into the world, he had to pick a family. That would mean
a young mother and father to raise him. When he chose
Mary, just think how humbled she must have felt. She was
favored not because of what she had already accomplished
but because of what God saw in her. He knew that she
would be the perfect pick, and that must have meant the
world to her.

You are also highly favored. God has placed a dream
in your heart. He has given you a plan for your life. He has
designed you to fulfill something great in life. He will give
you an audience to speak to, a job to do. And all because of
what he sees in you. You are highly favored, not because of
what you've already done but because of what God knows
you will do. He has selected you and perfectly placed you to
do what only you can do. Why would you stop now? There
is so much greatness ahead if you just hold on.

keep moving

What is one thing that is unique to you that God
is using?

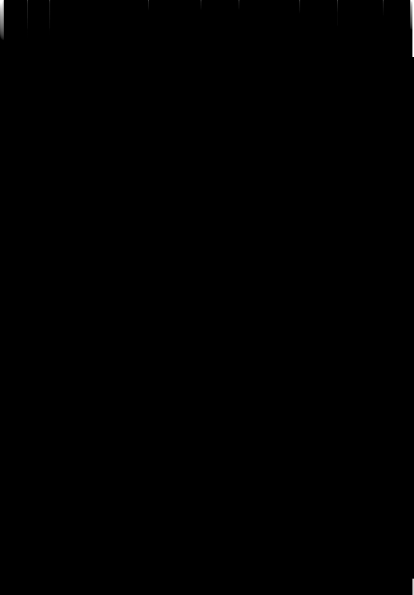

nothing is impossible

"Nothing will be impossible with God."

Luke 1:37 ESV

It was completely and utterly unbelievable. Inconceivable! To Mary, it was hard to understand how this word of the Lord could actually come to pass. After all, she was a virgin. And now she was going to be a mother? It seemed impossible.

But with God, all things are possible. There is nothing he has shown you that he does not have the power to make happen. There is no promise he has given you that he cannot fulfill. There is no vision that you won't one day see before your eyes.

Take your impossibilities and give them to God. While you are stuck wondering how, step back and watch God. Then move out knowing he has a firm grasp on the wheel. He is the one who parted an insurmountable sea. He is the one who multiplied dinner for over five thousand people. He is the one who won victory after victory. And he is the one who allowed a virgin to give birth. If he did all that, there is nothing he can't do for you.

keep moving

Make a list of your "impossibles" and give them to God.

the Lord's servant

"See, I am the Lord's servant," said Mary.
"May it happen to me as you have said."

LUKE 1:38 CSB

What was your response the first time you imagined what
the Lord was leading you to? When he placed that dream
in your heart, you had an immediate reaction. What was it?
One of fear? Or confidence? Of empowerment? Of doubt?
There are no right or wrong answers. But there is one
response that seems to be better than any other. "See, I am
the Lord's servant."

Being a servant of the Lord first takes submitting to
him. Putting your own feelings and desires behind those of
God's righteousness. Placing yourself under his control and
accepting that you are his servant.

But what about those servants? Aren't they second-
class citizens? Absolutely not! God loves you and cares for
you. As you humble yourself before him, he will respond by
exalting you and making you greater than you ever thought
possible. But the first step is to place yourself at the feet of
the Lord. Are you ready?

keep moving

What is one area of your life that you need to submit
to God?

the Holy Spirit is doing this

While Joseph was thinking about this, an angel from the Lord appeared to him in a dream. The angel said, "Joseph, the baby that Mary will have is from the Holy Spirit. Go ahead and marry her."

MATTHEW 1:20 CEV

Put yourself in Joseph's shoes for just a moment. You've been given what is the most incredible news and the most heartbreaking news—and it's the same news! The Messiah is coming to save the world! And your fiancée is pregnant. Those two things would cause you to experience feelings on opposite ends of the emotional spectrum.

But Joseph is immediately encouraged. An angel's visit squashes all rumor and innuendo. Mary is not pregnant by another man, but it is the Holy Spirit doing this. The power of God is overshadowing her. The Lord is sovereignly moving. This may be the only answer that would have calmed Joseph's fears.

Did you know the Holy Spirit is still moving in lives? In fact, he is moving in *your* life. He is the one who placed that dream from God in your heart. And he is the one who is empowering you to keep on going. Step after step, he is right there with you. No reason to doubt or fear. He's got this, and he's got you.

keep moving

What is one way you have felt the Holy Spirit move in your life this year?

Jesus will save his people

"She will give birth to a Son; and you shall name Him Jesus,
for He will save His people from their sins."

MATTHEW 1:21 NASB

Jesus came to save. That was his singular purpose. In every prophecy, every message, it was clear. In his very name is the reason he came to earth. He has come to save us from our sins. He has come to save us from insignificance. He has come to save us from our fear and doubts.

Names are very important in the Bible. Sometimes, God changes names to reflect a new reality. For Jesus, his name was very significant. That name comes from two different words in Hebrew. The first part of his name indicates a who: the Lord. The second part is the what: saves. His very name means "the Lord saves." What a name to have! What a name to put your trust in.

When you came to Jesus, he saved you from your sins. He turned you into someone who can overcome their past. But his salvation didn't stop there. Being saved means more than just punching a ticket for heaven. It represents your new abundant life. It tells you that you'll be all right. Every situation and struggle you come up against, he wants to save you from it.

keep moving

Make a list of things you have been saved from in your life.

the blessing of his words

"You are blessed because you believed
that the Lord would do what he said."

LUKE 1:45 NLT

What a great thing to believe the words of the Lord!
You can't seem to trust what you read online, see in the
newspaper, or hear on TV. But one thing you can believe in
is every word from the Lord. As you read your Bible, make
note of things that offer you hope and peace. And then
believe them.

Believe the word that comes to you too. God is here
to speak as long as you are here to listen. As you hear his
word to you, believe it. You will be blessed when you put it
into action in your life. The key to unlocking your destiny
is to be a receptive listener who is ready to move. Don't get
stuck wondering. Get moving by believing.

keep moving

What was the last word you heard from the Lord?

the hungry are filled

"He has filled the hungry with good things,
and sent the rich away with empty hands."

Luke 1:53 GNT

Are you hungry? Is your stomach growling? Has it been a while since you had a bite to eat? You may want to take a break right now and have some food.

But what about spiritually? Are you hungry for the things of God? Are you thirsty for the presence of the Lord? Are you hanging on every word that comes from his mouth?

God has promised to fill the hungry. He won't turn anyone away who has a need. That means he will meet every physical need. But also, every spiritual desire. You don't have to worry about leaving him empty-handed. He has prepared a table for you and can't wait to share it with you. And he knows that once you are filled, you will be ready to move out.

keep moving

What is your greatest spiritual hunger right now?

where is Jesus?

"Where is the newborn king of the Jews?
We saw his star as it rose,
and we have come to worship him."

MATTHEW 2:2 NLT

Wise men came to see Jesus. They wanted just to be in his presence. They had seen a star in the sky that told them he was on his way. They searched the Scriptures to find out just what this meant. And they came expecting to see him.

Are you expecting Jesus to show up today? You have needs and demands on you. Your schedule has to-dos that you must get to. Your mind may even be racing to put all these things in order. You don't know if you'll get it all done. But in the midst of that is Jesus. He will be there today, and you will meet him if you look for him.

As you go about your day, ask yourself, *Where is Jesus?* He may show up in line at the store; while you wait your turn, you feel his presence. He could show up at the most chaotic hour or a moment of serene downtime. He may show up in the smile of a stranger or the warm embrace of a friend. Search for him, and you will find him. Look for him, and he will appear. Ask for him, and he will answer.

keep moving

Be on the lookout for Jesus to appear to you today.

good news of great joy

The angel said to them, "Don't be afraid, for look,
I proclaim to you good news of great joy that will be
for all the people."

LUKE 2:10 CSB

What a wonderful time of the year! God has prepared this moment just for you. He has good news to share, and it will give you great joy.

There's not much news today that makes us happy. Every day you open the paper, scroll social media, or flip on the news, you will be confronted with reasons to mourn, to doubt, to grow angry. You will hear about death and destruction, of lies and deceit, of evil and tragedy. But God won't leave you that way. He will give you a reason to be happy. He will show you what true joy is all about.

The good news, also known as the gospel, is not just a story of Jesus' birth, life, and death on the cross. It's so much more. It's a never-ending story of his life in your life. It's how he connects with us. It's where he is leading us. You don't need to be stuck in an endless cycle of bad news. Instead, listen to the good news that brings great joy.

keep moving

Think of one aspect of the good news that gives you great joy.

glory to God

*"Glory to God in the highest heaven,
and on earth peace to those who have his good will!"*

LUKE 2:14 GW

Those shepherds were not expecting this: angels appearing in their field to announce the Messiah's birth. They probably thought they would be the last to hear something like this. Everyone else overlooked them, doubted them, excluded them. Then, in a moment, God's great light embraced them. God's glory surrounded them. They became the first witnesses to the greatest birth ever.

Glory to God! What a great thing he has done for you. He wants you to know. He wants to make you a witness. He is showing off, and you get a front-row seat. Just sit back and see how he will move in the next few days, weeks, and months to come. You have nothing to fear. He will lead you. And he will keep you heading in the right direction.

keep moving

What is something in your life that can bring glory to God?

far and wide

When they had seen him, they spread the word concerning
what had been told them about this child.

LUKE 2:17 NIV

The shepherds couldn't wait. It was late at night. The sky
was dark, the air crisp. They had worked all day before an
angelic choir interrupted their sleep. Now, after rushing
into the little town of Bethlehem to see the newborn Savior,
they were pumped. They were so excited! They couldn't
take time to sleep it off or wait another minute. They had to
let everyone know.

They ran from house to house, shouting and telling
their story. They woke up every last friend they had,
then started in on those they didn't even know. They told
everyone!

Who have you told lately about who Jesus is? It
doesn't take a three-point sermon or perfect theology. It
only takes recounting what has happened to you. That's
what these shepherds did. They told everyone what they
saw—angels with a message, a baby with a destiny. And
then they kept going.

keep moving

Stay unstuck today by sharing with others
about Jesus.

it's almost time

While they were there,
the time came for her to give birth.

LUKE 2:6 ESV

It's almost time. Christmas is almost here. Just one more day. Tonight is Christmas Eve, the holiest night of the year. We recognize this as the eve of the day the Lord was born. We gather with friends and relatives, read the Christmas story, and get to bed. Tomorrow we celebrate. We will exchange gifts and share joy. But tonight, it's time for waiting and anticipating.

In your life, there have been moments when you could say, "It's almost time." God's dream was coming true before your eyes. You knew you were so close; that promise he gave you was finally nearing reality. Today, take a moment to reflect on those times.

keep moving

Think of an "it's almost time" moment from this last year.

the greatest gift

God so loved the world that he gave his one and only Son,
that whoever believes in him shall not perish
but have eternal life.

JOHN 3:16 NIV

Merry Christmas! Today is the day when we open gifts and celebrate with family and friends. But God has already shared the greatest gift of all. There are so many ways to put it, but the best words are from the most famous verse ever: "God so loved the world that he gave his one and only Son."

When we put our whole trust in him, he gives us his whole promise. Jesus has fulfilled every promise the Father has ever given. Every prophecy and every message points to Christ. Your whole life has led up to you receiving that from him today. Gladly accept his gift.

keep moving

Share with someone today about how much Jesus means to you.

don't come empty-handed

Entering the house, they saw the child with Mary his mother, and falling to their knees, they worshiped him. Then they opened their treasures and presented him with gifts: gold, frankincense, and myrrh.

MATTHEW 2:11 CSB

The wise men did not come empty-handed. They traveled thousands of miles to see the baby King born in Bethlehem. And they were ready to meet him. They opened up from their personal treasure and gave freely to Jesus.

God has given you all you need. You have a treasure, a talent, and you have time. From those storehouses, you can give back to him. How? By giving to others. You see, there was only one time in human history that we could give a physical gift to baby Jesus. We've missed out on that time. But we can still give him a gift today. Every time we do something for the least of all, we do it as if to Jesus. Any gift you give, any service you provide, any grace you show to someone in need, you are giving it to Jesus. And that will provide fuel for your future even now.

keep moving

What is one way you can give to the needy today?

Wonderful Counselor

To us a child is born, to us a son is given, and the government will be on his shoulders. And he will be called Wonderful Counselor, Mighty God, Everlasting Father, Prince of Peace.

Isaiah 9:6 niv

Many people in the Bible have more than one name. There is Peter, who was also called Simon. Then you have Paul, who used to go by Saul. Jesus had more names than any other person. In this prophecy, we read about four of them.

First of all, Jesus is the Wonderful Counselor. He is wise beyond any human measure. That's what *wonderful* means: "above and beyond." And his wisdom is from the Holy Spirit. James told us that if any of us lack wisdom, we can simply ask the Father. The Father gave Jesus this wisdom as well. And Jesus applied it every day of his life on earth. He was aware of what was moving behind the scenes. And he used this wisdom to keep moving toward the goal God had placed before him.

We can also use this wisdom. When Jesus comes into our lives, he grants us wisdom beyond our own human ability. God will give you supernatural insights as he shares his wisdom with you. It should motivate you to move.

keep moving

Think of a time when you had wisdom beyond your own ability.

Mighty God

"The LORD your God wins victory after victory and is always with you. He celebrates and sings because of you, and he will refresh your life with his love."

ZEPHANIAH 3:17 CEV

Not only is our Lord ever wise, but he is also ever powerful. He is a mighty God. In the Bible, he is personified as a warrior, a hero in the battle, ready to save us. And he is always with us. His mighty hands guard us at all times. There is nothing to fear when we are sheltered underneath him. He will guide us through the most difficult moments of life.

As a mighty warrior, he will bring victory after victory in your life. And then, he will lead you in a time of celebration. You will hear his song singing over your life. You will be transformed by his refreshing Spirit. You will find his love leading you on.

The mighty warrior God wants you to know that you don't have to give up. You don't have to stop now when you're so close to your goal. Keep going because there is victory just ahead.

keep moving

Make a list of the victories God has given you this year.

Everlasting Father

Before the mountains were born or you brought forth the whole world, from everlasting to everlasting you are God.

PSALM 90:2 NIV

Not only is our God ever powerful, but he is also everlasting. The book of John tells us that Jesus was there before the world began. Then, at the end of the New Testament, John told us that Jesus will be there long after the world has ended and is renewed. From the beginning of time to the end, Jesus is above all and in all. He is guiding us through it all too.

Jesus is not held back by time. He comes at just the right time for you and me. He sees time differently than we do as well. He knows all and is all-powerful, so he puts into action his plan at just the right time. Though we may be impatient, he is patient with us. He is waiting for the right moment to share his love and life with us. If you are waiting on a miracle, know that Jesus has not forgotten you. Don't get stuck impatiently waiting for an answer. Move boldly into his bright future for you and your life.

keep moving

When was the last time you were impatient about God's work in your life?

Prince of Peace

"Peace is what I leave with you; it is my own peace that I give you. I do not give it as the world does. Do not be worried and upset; do not be afraid."

JOHN 14:27 GNT

Not only is God everlasting, but he is also ever present. His presence in your life is what gives you peace. It is what clears the path in your own mind. As sleepless nights come one after the other, as anxious thoughts seem to override your consciousness, God is there to grant you peace. His very presence in your life is a testament to the fact that he loves and cares for you, and he will grant you peace.

Peace comes in different forms for us. It can mean settling a dispute with a friend or relative. It can mean finally getting a clean bill of health. It can also be put into song to soothe our souls.

Peace can also mean rest. After a long year of chasing after your dreams, embrace the rest he gives. Your sabbath rest is just ahead. It's not a break from following God's will for your life. It's a moment to look back and see how great he has been and what he has ahead for you. Don't stop now! Your rest is within reach.

keep moving

What do you need to rest from this season?

light shines

The light shines in the darkness,
and the darkness has not overcome it.

JOHN 1:5 NIV

The last night of the year. A realization that you've made it.
And a hope for a better tomorrow. You'll start a brand-new
year with brand-new promises tomorrow. You might look
back in regret, but why? There is light in the sky tonight! A
great shining that disperses the darkness. Focus on the light.

God has done so much this year and has brought
you so far. Yes, there has been darkness, but that darkness
has not overcome you. In fact, you have answered every
challenge head-on. You have faced every struggle with
courage. You have answered every doubt with truth. You
have managed every heartache with grace. You have done
it! You are a winner!

keep moving

Record your greatest victory from this last year.

about the author

Tyler Feller is an author, pastor, and podcast host. He pastors Movement Church, a unique expression of the gospel that reaches people online and has members in all fifty states and twenty-two countries. He resides in Nashville, Tennessee, where he hosts encounter nights at which thousands have experienced a deep collision with God's love. The podcast he hosts is called *Deep Waters* and features some of the most popular figures in Christianity and pop culture as they talk about important cultural and spiritual issues. Tyler attended Global Awakening Theological Seminary and has a master's degree in business management. He is passionate about seeing people step into their design and destiny.